LOSING MY VOICE
AND
FINDING ANOTHER

Learning a Second Language

COOPER THOMPSON

MSI Press, LLC

Copyright 2011 by MSI Press, LLC

All rights reserved. No part of this book may be reproduced or utilized in any form or by any means, electronic or mechanical, including photocopying, re-cording, or by any information storage and retrieval system, without permission in writing from the publisher.

For information, contact:
MSI Press, LLC
1760-F Airline Hwy, 203
Hollister, CA 95023

Library of Congress Control Number 2011944901

ISBN 9781933455235

cover design by CDL Services

Printed in the United States of America

For Inge and Elisabeth

It is only because of you that I came here and learned this awful language. But I have no regrets. It was a good decision.

Table of Contents

Foreword .... *vii*

Acknowledgments .... *ix*

Prologue: An Unexpected Journey ....*xv*

PART 1:
Losing My Voice:
difficulties in learning and using a new language 19

    Regression 21
    Fear 33
    Anger 43
    Sadness 53
    Rules 67

PART 2:
Finding My Voice:
successes and challenges on the path to fluency 81

    First steps 83
    Confidence 95
    Recognition 107
    Confrontation 117
    Holding on 125
    Silence 137
    Ups and Downs 143
    Intimacy 157
    Trusting Myself 167

References 183

About the Author 185

Cooper Thompson

Foreword

I first met Cooper four or five years ago. When I heard that he had learned German as an adult, I immediately invited him to speak to my University of Maryland graduate class, which was composed of current and prospective language teachers from different parts of the world. For several hours, he entranced the class with his tale of falling in love with a German woman, getting married, moving from the United States to Germany, learning German, and acculturating to a very different style of life – all as a middle-aged adult. My students, who had learned foreign or second languages and had encountered new cultures, instantly related to his adventures. The students pelted him with questions about language learning and cultural adaptation, and he answered with great insight. The class period flew by. Everyone wanted to know more about his experiences than he could possibly share in our short time. Because of the need for many more people to know his story, I strongly encouraged Cooper to write this book.

This book confirmed for me that language learning is a truly an adventure of the body, mind, and spirit. As I wrote in the preface to my very first book, the characteristics that help learners become proficient in a new language and culture include: "A more practiced eye, a more receptive ear, a more fluent tongue, a more involved heart, a more responsive mind." The current volume reveals how an adult language learner, Cooper Thompson, developed such qualities. Far from being an idiosyncratic, purely individual tale, it has an almost archetypal meaning for anyone who has ever learned an additional language or who, as an adult, might want to consider learning one.

As shown in these pages, Cooper's adult journey in language and culture fundamentally rocked his world. In this volume, Cooper reveals the cognitive demands of serious adult language learning, such as the new mental frameworks he suddenly needed for organizing the vast waves of new vocabulary, grammatical structures, shades of meaning, and cultural practices. He examines the array of emotions tied to various events experienced while learning German: anxiety, excitement, anger, hope, contentment, confusion, and joy. He explores his own motivational ups and downs, a topic that less personal books on language learning fail to address adequately. He also probes the far deeper changes that language learning wrought in his identity, personality, relationships, and even life-purpose. When I read his words, my own world was altered. I entered a new dimension and gained fresh insights about the substance and the soul of language learning, even though I have been in the language field for decades.

In at least two ways this book fills a major gap in literature. First, no theoretical work on language learning can capture the depth of authentic experience that Cooper's book offers. Second, famous personal memoirs about language learning and cultural adaptation, such as *Lost in Translation* by Hoffman and *Hunger of Memory* by Rodriguez, often focus on how a child learns a language beyond the mother tongue and how he or she spends years learning to navigate across cultures and identities. Instead, this book starts in the adult years and focuses on experiences of a fully mature, professionally competent individual.

Because Cooper Thompson is a perceptive, lively storyteller, his reflections are rich, enlightening, and captivating. Because of his social and psychological sensitivity, he is able to provide useful information to readers of both genders and of a range of backgrounds. This important and eminently readable book will be a boon to language teachers, language learners, educational researchers, sociologists, and cultural experts, and it will be fascinating to ordinary readers who enjoy a good story.

Rebecca L. Oxford, Ph.D.
Professor, United States Air Force Culture and Language Center,
Montgomery, Alabama
Distinguished Scholar-Teacher and Professor Emerita, University of Maryland

Acknowledgements

Many people have helped make this book possible, including the following:

- my German teachers, especially Lee Riethmiller, Elke Hess, Judith Weibrecht, Harald Ruck, Esther Härtle, and Harald Bierlein-Neußinger;

- second language researchers and learners, especially Bonnie Norton, Madeline Ehrman, and Eva Hoffman, whose books I read and re-read, and who gave me ways to explain the difficulties I was experiencing;

- friends and acquaintances who reminded me that my German was good, or good enough, and encouraged me on my journey: Annette Becker, Henri Randriamanana, Walli and Uwe Müller-Glatz, Claudia Korman, Claudia and Marcus Speiser, Thy Ly Nguyen, Roland John, Martin Sossau, Karina Schindler, Tobi Dennerlein, Jesse Dröge, Stephan Weber, Sabine Schwarz, Jürgen Krank, Elzbieta Szczebak, Jean-Francois Drozak, Günter Ernst, Hans Joachim Lenz, Robert Katianda, Carmen Drinkmann, Jean-Pierre Muteba, Tilman Eckloff, ManuEla Ritz, Jürgen Schlicher, Jutta Seifert-Jammeh, Sabine Sommer, Gül Yoksulabakan, Rudi Herbig, Martin Häckel, Lisa Niebel, Regina Häring, Monica Lehnert, Eva Neuner, Gertrude Weidner, and Hannelore Zimmermann;

- people who accepted me into their circles, shared themselves, and gave me the opportunity to learn about myself, including members of the self-help group, the men's discussion group, the immigrant support group, the Jazzchor, participants in the Diversity Works Trainer Certificate Program, participants in the week long seminar in Toulouse, students in the FACE workshop, and participants in trips sponsored by Offene Behindertenarbeit;

- my neighbors in Höfles who welcomed me, and Jürgen Wolfel, Andi Weidl, Sebastian Heinze, Ludwig Ebenhack, and Günter Laus, great guys and great craftsmen;

- the women and men at the Hauptmarkt and the Friday Kobergerplatzmarkt, doctors and dentists and their assistants who treated me with respect, and strangers I met in daily life who gave me great material to work with;

- Rebecca Oxford, who invited me to teach in her class, told me she loved my manuscript, and supported me as I searched for a publisher;

- Yalun Zhou, who told me I was bilingual and put me in touch with MSI Press;

- Betty Leaver, the managing editor of MSI press, who saw the manuscript and offered me a contract right away;

- long-term mentors whose wisdom supported me as I learned German: Wekesa Madzimoyo who gave me a model for understanding feelings and showed me how to be myself despite what the dominant group thinks; Jo Lewis who taught me most of what I know about Transactional Analysis and helped me learn to trust myself; Valerie Batts who taught me about trusting the process through her words and actions; Gerald Jackson for reminding me (hell, gently insisting) that when I have something valuable, I need to share it; and my colleagues at VISIONS who helped me understand modern and internalized oppression;

- practitioners of Transactional Analysis for developing psychological models that helped me understand and respond to my experience; concepts from TA are scattered throughout the book;

- Ursula Flückiger and Fred von Allmen who shared their experiences using a foreign language and helped me accept my thoughts and feelings about German, and many other Vipassana teachers who taught me the power of practice and the wisdom of the Dharma;

- Melissa Lamson, Benjamin Zander, Gordon Murray, Suhith Shivanath, and Doug Baker who gave me valuable tips about learning a second language and living in Germany;

- Tsering Angduc for his wisdom and friendship;

- Marie and Bernard Dufeu who developed an extraordinary method for learning a language, Psychodramaturgie Linguistique (PDL), and my fellow students in the PDL Ausbildung in Mainz; Nadja Maffei who showed me the power of PDL and gave me a magic carpet ride into the world of Italian,

- Klaus Beutelspacher, Eveline Bruijn, Wendy Conklin, Meck Groot, Ingrid Gürtle, Doris Katheder, Regina Marvis, Dai Pritchard, Diana Santelli, Jürgen Schlicher, and Ruth Schmid, who read drafts of the book and gave me comments and encouragement; and

- most important, all the members of my wife's family, who accepted me as part of the family (Maybe it's time for me to stop saying "my wife's family," and instead say, "my family!").

Many of you didn't know that you were helping me write this book, but I couldn't have done it without you. Thank you!

This is a book about my personal experiences as I recall them. Because it is based on memory, it is probably not always accurate. But it is what I remember, and I have tried to write what I believe actually happened. This is especially true with dialogue. Almost all of the dialogue in this book took place in German, and yet I am writing in English. It is not possible for me to translate these dialogues word for word, nor do I think it is necessary. I have tried to communicate the spirit and style of the conversation with as much detail as I can remember. If I misrepresented what someone said, I apologize.

Especially in the first few years of living in Germany, I was very critical of German culture and German people. I was not able, or not willing, to understand their experience with immigrants and immigration and see things from their perspective. As a result, what I wrote about Germans and Germany isn't necessarily accurate or fair. When I wrote something critical, I intentionally changed some of the details to protect peoples' identities.

My wife suggested that I use pseudonyms, so I changed the names of family members and most of my German friends and acquaintances and other people with whom I had contact. I used the real names of Second Language Acquisition experts and a few other people where it was not a private conversation and could be valuable for the reader to know the real names.

"When we speak we are afraid our words will not be heard or welcomed. But when we are silent, we are still afraid. So it is better to speak."

> Audre Lorde, visionary, activist, and writer.

"My experience of marginalization was good for the soul and better for the intellect."

> Chandler Davis, speaking about the impact of being red-baited in the 1950's. Davis left the United States and has lived in Canada ever since.

"No one among the Mundo believes that there is anyone on earth who truly knows anything about why we are here. Even to have an idea about it would require a very big brain. A computer. That is why, instead of ideas, the Mundo have stories."

"You are saying, are you not," I said to Manuelito, "that stories have more room in them than ideas?"

Manuelito laughed. "That is correct, Señor. It is as if ideas are made of blocks. Rigid and hard. And stories are made of a gauze that is elastic. You can almost see through it, so what is beyond is tantalizing. You can't quite make it out; and because the imagination is always moving forward, you yourself are constantly stretching. Stories are the way that spirit is exercised."

"But surely you people have ideas!" I said.

"Of course we do. But we know that there is a limit to them. After that, story!"

By the Light of My Father's Smile, Alice Walker, p. 193-4

Prologue

An Unexpected Journey

I never thought I would live in Germany. I had dreamed of living in France, or Spain, or Italy. I spoke some French and Spanish, and I wanted to learn Italian. I could picture the sun, the food, the land. I could hear the melody in these languages. It seemed so romantic.

But Germany? Never. The image I had in my mind, based on old stereotypes I had picked up as a child, was a flat, grey industrial landscape where people spoke a guttural language that sounded harsh. During several trips to Europe as an adult, I had avoided Germany. And I had avoided challenging the stereotypes I had.

Unfortunately, I fell in love with a German woman—not the French or Spanish or Italian lover I had fantasized about. A few years later, she asked *me* to marry *her*. I initially said, "No," but with coaching from friends and a few sessions with a therapist, I came to my senses and said "yes." We got married in 2003.

I had planned to live out my life in the country where I was born and had always lived—the United States—in a house I had renovated, where I had family and friends, work that I found meaningful, people who valued what I did. But my wife and I decided to live in Germany. At the age of 53, I was suddenly faced with the challenge of beginning a new life in a new culture using a new language.

Starting over was not new for me. As an adult, I had already done that three times in different parts of the United States but never with a new language in a new country. The emotional pain I felt took me by surprise, and I felt alone in my pain. When I tried to explain my feelings, no one seemed to understand. And in truth, I didn't yet have the words to explain what was happening to me.

I had learned French and some Spanish when I was younger, and I enjoyed using these languages. But I didn't want to learn German. Learning German seemed more difficult than learning French and Spanish, and I didn't believe that I could do it.

Still, I made the decision to learn German. I fought with the language, and I fought with the culture. It was a constant struggle.

Many things contributed to making this difficult for me: the curriculum and teaching style in the classes I took, prejudices I had about Germany, what my parents taught me about language when I was as a child, and the fact that I am an older, white middle class man. Although living in Germany should have made the process easier—there were more opportunities for learning—I experienced it as pressure, as if I must learn and use German. It was completely different from using French and Spanish as an occasional tourist.

The teaching of German (and probably most foreign languages) focuses almost exclusively on words: what they mean, how they are used, how they are modified, how they are connected to each other in a sentence. But in my experience, learning another language as an adult has a lot to do with who we are, our conditioning, our social context, and how we actually communicate with each other. These things were not addressed in any of the classes I took.

There were times when I didn't want to hear German—it seemed too overwhelming—and times when I could listen to German but didn't understand and certainly wasn't ready to produce my own sentences. When children are first learning to talk, they seem to choose when they will practice, as if they need to trust the people around them to listen and take them seriously. Or maybe they are too shy, or it's just too hard to talk, or maybe they have nothing to say.

I felt all of these things. I was constantly confronted with what I didn't know and didn't understand. I couldn't communicate what I was feeling and thinking. I lost my sense of who I was. I lost my voice.

When I was a boy, my mother described me as a very sensitive child. It was not a compliment. As an adult, I am proud of my ability to express my feelings, and I have used that skill professionally. Nonetheless, because I had such strong emotional reactions to learning German, I thought something was really wrong with me.

One of my coping strategies was to keep a journal. It was a way to make sense of my experience. I also searched for information about the process of language learning. Eventually I found a few memoirs written by other people who had learned a second language, and later, I discovered that there was extensive research about second language learning.

The memoirs helped me know that I was not alone in my feelings, and the research confirmed my suspicions that learning another language is a complex process. Although the research is written in an academic style, and contradictory—experts disagree on how people learn a second language and on the best ways to do it—I found out that there were names and concepts for what I was going through, and that my experience was not unusual. Other people have the same difficulties.

In addition to the memoirs and research I found, I drew on resources that I had used in other parts of my life: a daily meditation practice, training in psychology, and an understanding of cultural differences and the dynamics of oppression. There were also people who supported me: my wife's family, who spoke German with me in a way I could understand; some German friends, who made the effort to communicate with me; and even strangers, like the cashier at a building supply store. One day she asked me where I came from and told me about her travels to the U.S. to visit a relative. After our first brief conversation, I always went to her register to pay, so that I could practice making small talk and remember that someone in this foreign country recognized me.

My desire to speak more than one language in a part of the world where it is common for people to be multi-lingual kept me going. It is still a mystery to me that people speak very different languages, using radically different sounds and structures, and yet are able to communicate about the same things that we all experience in life: weather, food, work, family, love. I wanted to be able to do that in German.

Now, in 2010, I consider Germany my home and plan to stay here. I live in the city of Nürnberg, in the state of Bavaria, where I have a full life and a circle of friends and acquaintances that includes Germans and other immigrants. I have been elected to a newly formed council of immigrants to help Nürnberg become a city where native Germans and immigrants from 165 countries can successfully live together.

I am still married—I have no regrets about that decision. I'm renovating a small weekend house in a village north of Nürnberg, where my neighbors and local craftsmen are friendly and generous. I have survived culture shock that seemed to last for years. I think I understand some things about German culture that I previously criticized, and I am slowly learning to accept what I can't change.

I haven't fallen in love with this language, and I now know that I will always be learning German. I will always have an accent and sound like someone whose native language is English. I will always make mistakes. That used to bother me but not anymore. It's who I am, and I'm doing the best I can.

This book is a seven year journey as I lose my voice and find another. It's not exactly a direct route. There are starts and stops, and sometimes I go over the same ground again and again.

And although it seems obvious to me now, I realized along the way that learning German was more than just learning a language. It was, and still is, an opportunity for me to learn about life, and about myself.

PART 1

LOSING MY VOICE:

difficulties in learning and using a new language

Regression

October 1, 2003

This morning my wife and I were married in the Standesamt, a municipal office on the main square in Nürnberg. It was a simple, formal process. We went back to our apartment for lunch with my new in-laws.

At 2 p.m., instead of going on a honeymoon, I walked across town and started a German course: Grundstufe 2, one level above absolute beginner, but still at the beginner level. I was in a class with fifteen other students. I didn't see anyone who looked like me.

I didn't understand what the teacher was saying. I didn't have the words to say what I was feeling and thinking. Although I was the oldest person in the class—I could have been the father or even grandfather of the other students—I felt like a child again, as if I were just starting kindergarten in the United States. I was lost and wanted to go home.

Why would I want to go through the pain of learning to do something I already mastered? I learned how to speak once in my life. Why would I want to do that again, even if it were another language?

I guess it had to be this way. As I learned this strange new language that didn't fit in my mouth, I became a child again. But I didn't like it. When I tried to communicate in German, I had very few words I could use, not the rich variety I had in English.

In the U.S., I was a teacher, a writer, and an activist. My life for almost thirty years focused on challenging various forms of oppression, like sexism, homophobia, racism, and xenophobia. I was absorbed in my work, and it affected how I thought about myself and everything I did, including the words I used. I learned to be cautious in my language and to look for subtleties in communication. But in German, I didn't know many words, and I certainly didn't understand nuances in the meanings of words.

What I did understand was my emotional reaction to hearing German. I didn't like the sound of it. It sounded flat and staccato, unlike French, which had melody and was soft in my ear. When I spoke French, I loved hearing the sound of it.

It wasn't just the sound of German that bothered me, it was the association I had with German. When I stood on the subway platform in Nürnberg and heard German men speak, I heard voices I first heard as a teenager in the mid-1960s. In world history class, we watched documentaries of Adolf Hitler speaking at the annual Nazi Party rallies in the 1930s. The films we saw were probably excerpts from *Triumph of the Will*, a propaganda film made by Leni Riefenstahl. I heard the power in Hitler's voice and watched people mesmerized by his presence, but I also knew the horror that this man would bring to the world. His voice represented evil to me.

I believe that hearing the voice of Hitler was my first contact with the German language. I didn't study German in high school. I took French.

Four decades later, I had chosen to live in the city where the Nazi Party rallies were held and where the Nürnberg laws were passed, laws that dictated the inferior status of Jews. A few years before I moved here, I had learned that some of my German ancestors were probably German Jews who emigrated to the U.S. almost a century before the Holocaust. Nürnberg had changed. There was a biennial celebration of human rights. There were large demonstrations against neo-Nazis. There was a culture of remembering so that the Holocaust would never be repeated. Still….

A Jewish woman from the U.S. who had lived in Germany for several years told me, "I don't want to learn German. I can't get past the fact that this is the language that was spoken by the Nazis."

No wonder I didn't want to learn German.

*****

It was because of Anna, my mother-in-law, that I decided to learn German.

Anna[1] was sad that her daughter had decided to marry a man from the U.S. who couldn't speak German. How would she be able to talk to her son-in-law?

---

[1] first names without a family name are pseudonyms of actual people; first names with a family name are real names of actual people

Anna loves to meet new people, ask questions, and through them learn about life outside of the small village where she lives, in the same farmhouse where my wife was born and grew up.

When my wife told me about her mother's reaction, I also felt sad. I wanted to be able to talk with her, too.

A few months before I moved to Germany, I decided to find a private tutor in Boston, where I lived at the time. I didn't tell my wife. I wanted to surprise her on my next trip over to see her. I only had a month before I'd be getting on the airplane, and I imagined arriving at the airport and being able to greet her and tell her about my flight, all in German. It turned out to be pure fantasy on my part.

I had heard of a man who claimed he could teach someone ten languages simultaneously. I wasn't sure if I believed that, but I was intrigued, so I called him. I explained how I didn't like the sound of German, that I didn't think it was possible for me to learn German, but that I wanted to be able to talk with Anna. He listened to me, seemed to understand, and was convinced that he could teach me German. We made an appointment to begin my lessons.

Although I couldn't have a conversation with Anna or my wife after ten private lessons, I did learn that my mouth was capable of making some of these strange sounds. I had fun, but it was the last time that I would enjoy a language lesson for the next six years.

My private lessons gave me enough confidence to sign up for classes in Nürnberg. I didn't yet believe that I could actually learn German, but I was willing to try.

Trouble is, signing up for a class to learn a language is not the same as learning a language. I sensed that this was one of the rare times in my life, at least as an adult, that I consistently heard a voice saying "You are not able to do this." For most of my adult life, I have had tremendous confidence in my ability to accomplish things. I have always believed that I could do something I hadn't done before even though I didn't know exactly how. I knew I would figure it out, but with learning German, I constantly told myself, "I can't do this."

My desire to talk with Anna got me to take the first step, but in reality, I didn't have enough contact with her to sustain my motivation. I only saw her a few times a year. Eventually, I would find other motivations: to make friends with Germans, to be able to participate in the cultural life of the city, to be able to attend workshops and groups, to feel comfortable living here. At this point, I had to find the energy each day to go to class. I had to make myself go.

I wondered if my resistance to going to class had something to do with being a student again. It had been a long time since I was in school, and when I finished my master's degree thirty years earlier, I decided it was the last time I would go to school. It just didn't fit my way of learning. I learned much more when I finally got out of school, so I told myself "no more schooling." Now I was back in school, and I didn't see any other way to learn German. There were other ways, but I didn't know that yet.

* * * * *

The other students in my class were between sixteen and thirty. I was fifty-three—clearly the oldest—and one of the few men. Most of the students were young women from Eastern Europe, the Middle East, South America, or Asia, taking this class so they could attend university, become qualified for employment, or reach a level of fluency required for citizenship. A few of them had children and were learning German so that they would be able to help their kids with school work. The two men in the class were learning German to improve their job chances. No one had registered for this class to improve their relationship with their mother-in-law.

There was a sixteen-year-old from China, who looked even younger than that. She had been in Germany for just a few weeks. I couldn't imagine myself at sixteen having the courage to live in a different country where I didn't speak the language. But here she was, learning German, a language vastly different from Chinese, and appearing to be learning faster than me.

One day, she and I were sitting next to each other; and that meant that we were going to be conversation partners when the teacher assigned an activity: talking about our everyday lives. In German there is a formal *you* and an informal *you*. We used the informal *you* in class, but from the little I knew about Chinese culture, I imagined that she was supposed to use a formal *you* with someone like me who could be her grandfather. If that was true, then she was breaking a cultural rule to be chatting with me as if we were peers. It was definitely awkward for me.

In this class, as in many language classes around the world, German was taught as if it was simply a body of knowledge that needs to be mastered. We studied grammar and learned vocabulary. There was a written curriculum that teachers were expected to follow. Although some teachers offered a variety of activities for different learning styles, this class seemed designed for students who wanted to pass a standard test to demonstrate their fluency.

The teachers in these classes had a tough job. Students came with different needs, different learning styles, different educational backgrounds, and different expectations of what a teacher does and what happens in a classroom. There was no common language for explaining concepts and giving instructions, so everything had to be communicated in German.

In this setting, I didn't expect that my needs would be completely met. But I was not interested in learning German so that I could pass a test. I was only interested in learning this language for social use. And in any case, my emotional response to learning German was so strong that I sometimes spent more energy dealing with that than with learning German.

My age was not just a social factor in this class; it was also a biological reality that set me apart from the younger students. My brain was not as flexible as it had been when I was younger. I heard a new word, learned the definition, heard the same word the next day, and couldn't remember what the word meant. I needed lots of repetition, and even with that, six months later I might forget the word.

I seemed to need extra time to process what I heard in conversation before I could understand and respond. Sometimes it was only a split second and sometimes a few minutes before I understood what was being said to me. This gap between hearing and comprehending didn't exist for me in English, or at least I wasn't aware of it. It was embarrassing, especially if I didn't know the people I was talking with. To account for this time lag, I would tell people, "Sometimes I'm a little slow in German. I need a bit more time to understand." It was self-deprecating, a way for me to make light of the situation. This became one of my German survival phrases that I created and used frequently.

One day, as I rushed to class, I ran into an older immigrant from Croatia who worked for a plumbing contractor in my neighborhood. He and I had greeted each other on occasion. We didn't say much, but I felt a warmth between us.

"Where are you going?" he asked me.[2]

"My German class. But it's hard."

"German was hard for me, too."

---

2   All dialogue in this book originally was in German, unless noted; all dialogue with my wife was in English.

"But I have to learn German. And I'm late."

He paused, looked at me like a grandfather who loved me, and said, slowly, "Langsam junger Mann, langsam."

His words become a mantra for me when I felt frustrated: "Slow down, young man, slow down."

* * * * *

Learning a new language involves making lots of mistakes. But as a child, when I made a mistake in speaking English, my father would correct me. He didn't do it gently.

He was tougher with my older sister; looking back, I would now say that he was abusive. It was worse if he had been drinking, which happened every day when he came home from work. Cocktail hour began promptly at 5 pm, earlier on weekends.

I remember my father sitting with my sister at the kitchen table one evening, "helping" her with her math homework. She was maybe nine years old, and I was about six. She didn't understand what he was explaining. She got scared and began to cry. Then he got angry with her for crying and told her she was stupid. I don't know how often this happened, but it was not a one-time event.

I can easily imagine my six-year-old brain deciding "If I don't understand things, I'll get into big trouble." So I learned how to listen and observe very carefully, and I decided to try to understand everything and act like I was smart. If I could do that, then I would avoid his wrath and feel safe in the house.

Sometimes as I sat in German class, I felt an old fear as if my father were standing right behind me. And I thought, "I have to understand." Of course, the purpose of my being here was to learn what I didn't yet know. It was not possible for me to completely understand this language, not yet, maybe never. But sometimes I couldn't think clearly because my emotional reaction was so strong.

In class one day, I was in a practice conversation with a man from the Ukraine who knew more German than I did. We were role-playing. He was the guest and I was the manager at a hotel. He was complaining that the *Fahrstuhl* wasn't working. I did not know this word, and I would have sworn that I had never heard it.

I asked him what *Fahrstuhl* meant, and I heard him say something that sounded like "leaf." I didn't know that word either. He had a look on his face that I interpreted as "What's wrong with you that you don't understand what I'm saying?" It wasn't exactly a mean or angry or judgmental look, but it wasn't a loving and kind and seeking to reassure me look, either.

Suddenly I felt my face get hot, and I had a sensation of being temporarily lost. I stopped thinking, and I was overwhelmed by fear. It only lasted about five seconds, and then I had the presence of mind to ask the teacher what *Fahrstuhl* meant. She gave me a synonym that I understood: *Aufzug*. Elevator.

As soon as I understood what *Fahrstuhl* and "leaf" meant, I was able to come back to the role-play and actually have fun. He and I created a dramatic scene for the class: he was complaining about everything, and I was telling him he was crazy. We were over the top in our acting, and by the end of the role-play we were laughing together.

A week or so later, as I wrote about this experience in my journal, I realized that the heat I had felt in my face had something to do with shame. It was what I felt as a boy when my father got angry with me for not knowing something that I couldn't have known. Although that happened a long time ago, the sense that I am "stupid" persisted, as a quasi-belief in my head and as a physical sensation in my body.

I also realized that my fellow student probably wasn't mad at me when I didn't understand him. The expression on his face, which I interpreted as judgmental and angry, could have been puzzlement at why I didn't understand. Or maybe he thought there was something wrong with how he was pronouncing *Fahrstuhl*, or that he had the wrong word.

It is years later, as I am writing this, that I think I understand why he used the word "leaf" as a synonym for elevator. He was trying to use English, and the word he knew for elevator was the British word for elevator: *lift*.

* * * * *

I got to know a few Germans. I wasn't ready to call them friends. We didn't have a shared history, and it didn't feel easy or supportive. It felt like work to be with them. I got nervous before we would get together; and when we did meet, I worked hard to understand what they were saying and worked hard to make myself understood.

I was a little paranoid that they didn't really want to talk with me and were simply doing this as a favor. Or maybe they were interested in me because I was somehow exotic. And yet there were moments when I enjoyed getting together; it was definitely filling my need for social contact. I was lonely.

Berndt, for example. I met him when my wife and I had dinner with some of her friends. We met a couple of times at Café Fatal, a quiet coffeehouse around the corner from where I lived. Berndt and I had a lot in common: we were about the same age, we had some of the same interests, he had thought about what it means to be a man, and he was serious and self-reflective like me. He asked questions and paid attention to what I was saying. Being with him eased some of the loneliness I felt.

I was glad to be meeting with Berndt; he reminded me of male friends I had in the U.S. But I was also aware of a fundamental inequality in our relationship based on language difference. It seemed to me that I had to work much harder than he did to stay in the conversation. When I did say something, I was less able to explain things, to express my thoughts, to share my feelings. It was easy for me to think he didn't understand me when I said something. As a result, I asked a lot of questions and listened, rather than talking.

So, I was reluctant to ask him to get together with me. As much as I wanted friends here, I felt like the shy, insecure boy that I once was: not knowing how to make friends, not feeling confident in my friendships, wondering if other people really wanted to have me as a friend.

I also felt this in my German classes. I noticed that I was not as social as the other students. They went to the café together for coffee; I stayed in class and studied. They went out to bars at night together; I stayed home. I was older and different.

The content and activities in our curriculum were based on life in Germany and sometimes our home countries. The topics were school, nightlife, fashion, and popular culture: topics that were interesting for the younger students in my class. But not for me. I was interested in other things.

So, I didn't feel motivated to participate in class. I asked myself: do I have anything to say? This sounds similar to something I experienced as a child—wondering if it's worth speaking.

I also asked myself: How am I going to learn this language if, in the process of trying to learn it, I keep feeling like I don't belong? Why would I pick up a German newspaper if I could barely read German? Why would I try to have conversations with my German neighbors if we couldn't communicate? Why would I go to class if I felt "stupid"?

If other adult immigrants were having a similar experience, then I can easily understand why they might want to stay within their own community, where they can speak their native language. I assume that they, too, don't want to feel ashamed of not being able to do basic, everyday things that they can do in their native language.

My own experience of feeling ashamed would occasionally return over the next few years. Even after I became reasonably comfortable using German, and was able to express myself in German, there were moments when I felt ashamed that my German was not good enough.

* * * * *

I didn't have peer models or friends of my age to support me in the learning process. I didn't have people who could tell me that my experience was normal. I felt stuck in the role of being a student and believed I had to go to class. I didn't know that I had choices for how I could learn this language.

Years later, I met Madeline Ehrman, an expert on second language learning difficulties. She suggested to me that I could have negotiated with my German teachers for what I wanted. It seemed so obvious. I had first learned to do this in college in 1969 and had done this many times in my life as a learner, and as a teacher and workshop facilitator I had regularly asked students and participants to tell me what they wanted. But it had never occurred to me to do as I was learning German.

Looking back, I realize how powerless I felt. I was scared, my self-esteem plummeted, and I didn't see options for solving this problem. But I wasn't conscious of being powerless in the sense of being able to talk about it and name it. I just felt it, and I reacted as if I really were helpless.

What I needed was an approach to language learning that would allow me to take on this complex task of language learning in the same way that children do. They listen and mimic and eventually create their own words, phrases, and sentences. They play with the language. They don't think about being powerful; they simply act like they are. And they don't think about their mistakes, until they get to school and teachers begin to criticize them.

I needed an adult version of this. I needed opportunities to experiment with the sounds of German, to move my body while I was trying to speak German, to use the language as best I could, without worrying if was right or not. I needed a minimum of correction and lots of repetition and lots of freedom to say whatever I wanted to say, at my own pace.

In class one day, the teacher asked us to talk about some cultural differences between our home countries and Germany. A Japanese woman told the class about an unwritten cultural rule against nose blowing in public, and how she had changed her behavior to accommodate German culture, where nose blowing is acceptable.

I interrupted her and started talking about the health implications of nose blowing. I had recently read an article that suggested that blowing your nose tends to increase ear infections. As I was rambling on and trying to figure how to say this in German, I was aware that the teacher looked impatient. If I had put words to her facial expression, she might have said, "Cooper, that isn't relevant to what we're talking about." But I just kept talking until I was satisfied that I had explained the danger of nose blowing. I doubt that anyone understood me.

After class, I thought, why in the world did I talk about snot and bacteria? And why did I ignore the teacher's subtle attempt to quiet me? It wasn't so awful what I did—I didn't hurt anyone's feelings, or cause a major problem for the class, or violate a cultural taboo—but I felt embarrassed about it.

My behavior was similar to what happens during sharing time in kindergarten when kids will say some really random things that have no connection to what other kids have shared. Maybe I just wanted to hear my own voice, to show off that I could say something. My German teachers always told us, "Practice, practice, practice."

When I told a friend about this—his daughter was five—he laughed, knowing exactly what I meant. She did this all the time, and he had found himself doing the same thing when he was learning Italian. Whenever he could, he'd try to use his Italian, even if it was out of context or inappropriate. Showing off and making random comments for the sake of practice is a learning strategy that I would continue to use as I learned German.

Several years later, I was talking with a friend who is originally from Poland and has lived in Germany for many years. She was telling me about an event she organized for her job and how pleased she was that the mayor was able to attend at the last minute because of a cancellation in his schedule.

"Ich habe Schwein gehabt," she exclaimed.

I must not have heard her correctly, so I interrupted her. "What was that you just said about a Schwein?"

"Ich habe Schwein gehabt." I quickly translated this in my head. I had heard her right. She did say, "I have had pig."

"What does that mean?"

"That I was lucky. You don't know this expression?"

I laughed and acted outraged. "No, I never heard this. And it's crazy. What does luck have to do with pigs?"

"I don't know. I'm not German. It's just a German expression."

Despite how ridiculous it sounded to me, I decided to incorporate this phrase into my vocabulary because it was kind of cool. Or so I thought. Over the next few days I found many occasions to use it. Unfortunately, my wife overheard me using it, and most of the time told me that the way I was using it made no sense.

After about a week of hearing about the pig I have had, my wife gave me a look when I again told someone, "Ich habe Schwein gehabt." I have stopped using the expression, but I haven't forgotten it.

Fear

Soon after I began Grundstufe 2, I wrote in my journal, "I feel so scared. I'm scared of not being understood, of not understanding, of not knowing, of not being able to say what I am thinking and feeling. I don't trust my ability to cope with the foreignness of everything here. How long will it take me to learn this language? Will I be able to have a real conversation in German? Will I ever feel comfortable with this language?"

I found a book that I thought might help me: *How to Learn Any Language* by Barry Farber. It didn't take long before I realized that this was not the book for me. On page 5, I read, "Follow the steps herein, and you *will* learn the language of your choice *quickly, easily, inexpensively, enjoyably*, and *on your own*." Those are *his* italics; I guess he really believes what he wrote. I didn't believe him at all, and in fact, I experienced his encouraging comments as a discount of what I was going through. He obviously hadn't experienced the pain that I knew; he seemed to have a natural ability for language learning. Or else he was in denial, or he was exaggerating. In any case, I couldn't identify with what he had written.

I am sure that there are people who read the same book and found it inspiring and useful. And there were people in Grundstufe 2 who seemed to have a natural ability to learn German and didn't suffer like I did. They learned German "quickly, easily, and enjoyably" just like Barry Farber. But there are also people who don't seem to have the ability to learn a second language, even though they try. And the rest of us are in between, learn at our own pace, and have a variety of feelings about the process.

Several years later, a veteran foreign language teacher told me, "It can take decades to learn another language. The problem with adults is that they think they can accomplish this in a matter of months by simply taking classes or buying a set of CDs and studying at home."

When I heard this, I thought that maybe I hadn't been such a bad language learner after all. But when I started going to class, I didn't know it would take so long and require so much effort.

To compensate for my fear and lack of confidence, I did things that I knew how to do in the U.S., ordinary things, like cooking a meal. I wanted to do something that was familiar. I enjoy cooking. Experimenting with German foods was a way for me to remember that I was capable of something.

My wife invited some of her friends to dinner. I cooked but couldn't join the conversation. Sometimes I escaped to the kitchen to wash dishes, where I re-energized myself for another half hour at the dinner table. Three hours of having people in our apartment and trying to understand German was my limit. After that, I wanted to crawl into bed.

When my wife and I visited her parents or siblings, or when we went to someone's house, and I knew that we would be using German, my first question to her before we even got there was, "When will we be leaving?" Because my wife has a tendency to try to please everyone, she wouldn't give me a clear answer. I got angry with her ambivalence, but actually, I was afraid that I would be trapped in a situation and couldn't get out.

Of course, it was never as bad as I imagined it was going to be. That's the nature of fear. It was work for me to listen to German, and sometimes it was even okay, maybe boring, but I got through it.

I was confused, too, about how much social contact I really wanted. I enjoy and need time alone, and it seems that my need for time alone is increasing as I grow older. At the same time I get energized from contact with people, if I find the conversation stimulating. I'm also picky about who I spend time with, and I didn't meet many people here who I wanted to spend time with.

Sometimes I listened to National Public Radio from the U.S. on the internet. It was a relief to hear English on the radio and understand what was being said. I needed this from time to time: the familiarity of my native language. Surprisingly, I heard a couple of reports about learning a second language.

One day, I heard a psychologist say that infants are soothed when they hear their mother tongue and scared by "foreign languages." A middle aged English woman I met, who had been in Nürnberg less than a year, described German as "a wall of sound" that overwhelmed her. Maybe she and I were experiencing the same fear that children experience.

On another day there was a program about ambient noise, that it makes us "dumber." Some researchers found out that we can't think as clearly or as quickly when we are surrounded by lots of music or voices or noise, for example in a restaurant. In our native language, we have the ability to "fill in" words that we don't hear or don't understand, so it is not necessary for us to hear every word for comprehension. But we can't do this as easily in a second language, certainly not when we are beginners, and certainly not if there is competition from music and other conversations.

I was happy to hear this information.

* * * * *

For three years prior to moving here, I had been consulting for a company in Boston, helping them create a workplace environment that respected cultural differences. When I told them that I was leaving the U.S. and would need to stop working with them, they wanted me to continue and suggested that I commute from Germany. I had never considered this and was skeptical that it would work, but I said I would give it a try.

So I flew to Boston almost every month and stayed for up to two weeks. They were satisfied with my work, and I got what I needed: being recognized and valued for my knowledge and skills. Plus, I used the trips to visit my parents and friends.

It was a relief and a privilege to travel back home. Some immigrants can afford to travel to see their relatives, others don't have the money even to leave Germany, and some asylum seekers are not even allowed to leave the city where they live. My travel expenses were paid, and because I was traveling so frequently, I got upgraded to business class after the first year. The rich get richer. It felt uncomfortable to be sitting in the elite section—I didn't think I belonged there—but it was nice to be sitting where I could have some peace and quiet.

When I told people in Germany that I flew to the U.S. for work, some were impressed. I must have had an important job for an employer to fly me over every month. My mother-in-law had a different reaction: she just shook her head. She had never been on an airplane and had no desire to fly. She thought I should stay on the ground.

After about 35 trips back and forth over the Atlantic, I would agree with her.

Because of my travel, I was not getting very far in learning German. I registered for a second course, Grundstufe 3 (basic level 3), but I missed half of the classes. So I asked Karuna, the teacher of my first German course to tutor me. We had become friends, and through her I met her husband, Matho. He's from India, and he was also learning German. He didn't like the language either. He preferred using English with me. I would go to their apartment, chat and drink tea with him, and then get private lessons from his wife.

Karuna and I met every day when I was in town. She prepared material based on what I wanted to learn and what was interesting to me. She found things that I might be able to read, gave me grammar exercises based on what I needed, and we had conversations about living in Nürnberg. I felt like I was making progress, and most of the time I felt comfortable with her.

But I also noticed that my anxiety never really left me. When I couldn't find the words to express something, I felt my face get hot and I had a sense that I was momentarily lost. When she corrected my mistakes, I felt embarrassed. I knew it was her job to do that, but my emotional reaction would take over, and I couldn't take in the information she was trying to give me.

One day, she was trying to explain something to me, I told her I didn't understand, and she again tried to explain it. I still didn't understand and asked her again to explain it. But when she tried the third time, I thought I heard some tension in her voice. This time I told her that I understood what she had been trying to explain to me even though I didn't understand. I didn't want her to get angry.

As I rode my bike home, I remembered that this was the old pattern I learned as a boy when I watched my father "teach" my sister: I believed I had to understand what he was saying, and if I didn't, then I should act like I did. Years later, as I got to know Karuna better, I realized that she was probably getting impatient with herself, scared that her teaching wasn't good enough. Both of us, in our own ways, were afraid.

I had a break in my work schedule in Boston for a couple of months, so Karuna suggested that I repeat Grundstufe 3. The class would be co-taught by Regina and Uta. Karuna knew both of them and thought they would be a good fit for me. Regina would teach on Monday and Tuesday, Uta on Wednesday and Thursday.

The first two days went well. Regina seemed to care about students. She learned our names quickly, chatted with us on breaks, and tried to find out what we wanted and needed. I felt pretty confident.

On Wednesday I arrived about a half hour late for class, and Uta was leading an exercise in the middle of the room. The other students were standing in a circle. Uta noticed me, told me to join the circle, and without asking my name or introducing herself, gave me instructions for the exercise she was leading. I didn't understand what she was asking me to do, and I asked her to repeat her instructions. She did, but what I mostly heard was the tone of her voice, and I saw a slight frown on her forehead. That communicated more to me than what she was actually saying, and like my experience with Karuna, I believed that Uta was irritated with me.

Unfortunately, I still hadn't understood her instructions. I asked her again to repeat herself, and this time it was worse: she really did appear to be irritated. It wasn't just subtle changes in her voice and expression. I felt my whole body getting hot. I became speechless. I simply shook my head to indicate that I didn't understand. She shook her head, too, which I interpreted as, "You're hopeless," and moved on to another student. At the break, I left the class and never returned on the days that she was teaching.

Regina asked me the following week what had happened. Apparently Uta had told her that I left class without explanation. Regina spoke some English, and I tried to explain what I was feeling in Uta's class, but I felt a little foolish in my explanation. Here I was, a grown man who had gotten so scared by a small gesture from a teacher that I had refused to go back to class.

A year later, in another class, I talked to students who had had similar experiences with Uta. So it wasn't just me.

I know that Uta's job was to teach, which meant giving instructions, organizing activities, and repeating things when we didn't understand. I know that she may not have been familiar with the research on emotional aspects of language learning. Like most German teachers (and maybe language teachers around the world), she was not trained to deal with feelings. She was trained, and expected in the German system, to teach us the technical aspects of the language, and she was not paid well for what she did.

I know also that my feelings were *my* problem. And yet Uta, in effect, ignored something that is a core part of my identity: my feelings. I was scared yet trying my best, and she criticized me for not being good enough. The message to me was, "Cooper, there is something wrong with you." This same thing happens to students day in and day out in schools everywhere with the same impact: they believe that there is something wrong with them.

A couple of years later, my wife told me about an experience she had had when she was a teenager, an experience that still makes her angry when she recalls it. She grew up on a farm learning and using a dialect of German called Oberpfälzisch, but in school, she was expected to use standard German. She has a strong emotional connection to her dialect. It is the language she uses with her family.

One day she was giving an oral report in front of the class. She used Oberpfälzisch instead of standard German. The teacher told her that the content of the report was good, but gave her a bad grade simply because she used dialect. My wife was angry. She felt the teacher's comments as a discount of her identity, as if people who come from the village are inferior.

And it is still the case in Germany that teachers expect students to use standard German. People may not say it directly, but there is a wide spread belief that "educated people" should use standard German, also called high or formal German. Dialect is for country people.

* * * * *

About 15 years ago, I came across the following in a book called *The Roar of Silence* by Don G. Campbell. He begins a chapter titled *The Wounded Listener: Balancing Inner and Outer Sounds* by quoting an anonymous eighth grader in Liberia:

> Words cannot always be trusted. Words mean too many things to different people. If I listen with my feelings, then I understand what others really know about life. If I listen without my feelings, then I understand what others know about things. My teachers grade me on things. I do not think they remember how to listen to feelings. All of this confusion about learning and grades! My grandmother taught me that feelings were more important than facts or things because with them I'm connected to my life spirit and my ancestors and all the animal helpers.
>
> Most of my teachers and friends do not remember that words alone are not enough. So I do not trust the way others hear my thoughts. I can listen to their words and their hearts, but they do not understand my language. I think I'll be quiet until I can be heard without words. It's easier to communicate by drumming and singing. (p. 30)

I copied this and put it on the wall over my desk. It was a reminder to me of how important my feelings are.

Unfortunately, a language for expressing feelings was not included in my German classes. And from what I could see, feelings are not expressed directly or publicly in German culture, at least not in a way that I recognized. And it seemed that facts are more important than feelings; feelings are too subjective to be trusted. But like the young person in Liberia, I trust my feelings. Not as being more valid than facts, but as having equal value.

As a result, I felt discounted when I tried to express my feelings here in German with native German speakers. They didn't respond, or they seem puzzled by what I said, or they responded in a way that I interpreted as, "There is something wrong with me." Like the eighth grader in Liberia, sometimes I chose to be quiet until I could be heard.

*****

In the fall of 2004, a year after I had married and moved here, my mother was diagnosed with cancer. She died in November. My father died a year later in December 2005. For over a year, I spent more time caring for them in New Jersey than being with my wife in Nürnberg. Then in 2006, I traveled to Boston monthly for work and also to London every month for a seminar.

I had almost no time for myself. Even if I was in Germany for two or three weeks, I certainly didn't want to study German. I wanted to rest. I wanted to spend time with my wife. Or I needed to prepare for the next trip to Boston, or I was on the phone arranging care for my parents or dealing with the aftermath of their deaths. One time I flew back to Germany for the weekend, just so I could see my wife and sleep in my own bed.

Before I knew it, another year had passed, and it was late 2006. According to the calendar, I had been living here since the fall of 2003, but I had spent more time in the U.S. than in Germany. In hindsight, I suspect my traveling was a way to avoid settling here. Yet, I am grateful that I had so much time with my parents before they died, and I appreciated having paid work.

Somehow in those three years, I managed to complete three classes, meaning that I had achieved a basic level of German. It wasn't easy; I also had to repeat Grundstufe 4, and I continued to feel more uncomfortable than comfortable in class. But I made progress.

At the beginning of 2007, I decided to follow my mother-in-law's advice and keep my feet on the ground. I was so tired of traveling. I would have to go to Boston in the fall to finish up some work, but for nine months I would be able to focus on being here. I wasn't eager to keep going to classes, but I wanted to improve my German. So I registered for an intensive course at the intermediate level. I had finally graduated from being a beginner and was ready to take courses at the next level. Like before, I would be in class from 9 a.m. to 1p.m., four days a week.

The course was again led by Regina, and this time her co-teacher was Astrid. I talked to Regina before registering and she assured me that Astrid was not like Uta. My first impressions of Astrid were positive; she seemed respectful, engaging, and wanted us to succeed. I was feeling optimistic.

On the first day, I checked out the other students, as I always did. And as always, I was the oldest, but there was another middle aged man, and the younger people seemed friendly. I thought, maybe I'll like this class: good teachers, nice students.

The class was pretty successful, with one exception. I noticed that I often had a slight feeling of nausea as I went to class and walked up the two flights of stairs to the classroom. About halfway through the course, I began to have irregular heartbeats. It was a scary feeling when I suddenly noticed that my heart had skipped a beat or sped up without apparent cause.

I went see a doctor, took some tests, and managed to replicate the irregularity. It seemed that stress was causing this, and the only possible cause that I could see was my German class. The doctor prescribed something to treat the symptoms, but I didn't want to take medication. I wanted to reduce the stress, but I didn't want to stop going to class. I had to find a way to deal with my fear.

I asked my friend Doug Baker, a psychotherapist in the U.S., to help me. We created some "reminders to myself" to use when I would need to speak German. I wrote these down and posted them above my desk where I studied German at home. The list included the following:

- Making mistakes is normal, it is how we learn.
- It's okay if I don't understand something, I can ask for help.
- My goal is to continue learning and to practice speaking, not to speak perfect German.
- I don't need to rush, I can speak slowly and take my time, and the words will come to me.

The list also included meditation. I started meditating in 1995. I went regularly to a local mediation center before I moved here, but it had been hard for me to find a routine here. There was no group to sit with, no center to go to. I was having trouble finding the discipline to practice on my own in our apartment.

So in the spring of 2007, I attended a week long Vipassana meditation course at Seminarhaus Engl, a retreat center in the southeast corner of Bavaria. In its most basic form, Vipassana involves noticing what is happening in the present moment and accepting things as they are, without comparing, without judging what is better or worse. It was exactly what I needed as an antidote to my fears.

The leaders of the retreat, Ursula Flückiger and Fred von Allmen come from Switzerland. I talked with them about my struggle learning German and found out that we share something in common: they consider German to be a second language for them, too. Swiss German is their native language. They learned German in school and describe it as being imposed on them, as if their teachers believed German was superior to the Swiss German they grew up speaking. Fred told me that he would rather speak English than German. Once I knew this, I noticed them stumbling from time to time as they used German in the retreat. I appreciated seeing them make mistakes like I did.

They helped me see connections between meditation and language learning: the goal is to go deeper, to practice. There will always be more to learn. There are peaks, valleys, and plateaus. There is no end, no point at which I say, "I'm finished." I can work with what I have and with what is happening, not with what I should be able to do. I can remind myself: my German is enough for this moment, we communicated. If I don't understand something, it will be okay. Nothing bad will happen. My father can't hurt me.

I also realized that meditation was an antidote to my habit of comparing my language ability to others' ability. When I started a new German course or met another immigrant, I immediately tried to assess their German and find out who was better. It was rare that I met someone who had less ability than I did, so I usually concluded that my German was worse.

But what exactly do better and worse mean? I could have taken a standard test, gotten a score, and measured myself against others. A test like that, however, would have only measured certain types of technical, cognitive abilities, for example, which grammar rules I had learned, or which words I had memorized. It would not have measured my ability to use German in a conversation.

I doubt that there is a test that would have given me high marks for my courage in trying to talk with vendors at the market. Or the relationship I was trying to have with my mother-in-law when I called her on the telephone and wished her happy birthday, and tried, awkwardly, to have a conversation. Or my interest in listening to programs on Bayern 2, one of the public radio stations in Bavaria, even though I didn't understand much of the content.

Instead of comparing myself to others, I tried to stay focused on one question: "What do I want to learn?"

I found the strength to resume a daily meditation practice and it made a difference: I re-discovered some confidence and peace in myself. When I was in situations where I would be using German, and began to feel anxious, I focused on my breath. It took effort and repetition, and I was successful only part of the time, but my fear gradually diminished. Speaking German became an opportunity for me to practice acceptance of the way things are.

Anger

In the summer of 2004, about nine months after I had moved here and started learning German, my wife asked me to come along on a trip she was taking to northern Germany. Her job was to organize vacations for adults with disabilities. I would be one of several volunteers, and my job was to drive a van. We would be sightseeing and living together for a week, a temporary community of disabled and non-disabled people.

This was a stretch for me. I hadn't spent much time with people with disabilities, and it was not easy for us to communicate. My German was limited, and most of them had limited verbal ability. On the other hand, this was a bit of an equalizer. As I got to know the participants on the trip, we found ways to communicate. In some ways, it was easier for me to be with them than with non-disabled Germans.

Take Helga, for example. She was a very sensitive and compassionate woman who seemed to accept whatever came her way. At least once a day, she asked me how I was. I would tell her as best as I could, and she seemed to understand what I had said. I sensed that she understood, too, my discomfort with the language.

Or Fritz, a sweet man who always wanted to sit in the front passenger seat. He got agitated if he couldn't sit there. I don't know why this was; he didn't talk, or at least not in a way that I could understand. But somehow he communicated his feelings and needs, and somehow I understood him. I had a sense that he felt comfortable with me.

In contrast to Helga and Fritz, one of the volunteers on the trip, Maria, was bossy and patronizing. Rather than treating the participants the way my wife did—as adults with freedom to make their own decisions—Maria treated them like children, making decisions for them. I grew really irritated at meal times when I watched her cut the meat on their plates, like a parent would do for a child. They hadn't asked for that and didn't need her to do that. I watched them try to avoid her, but because she had some responsibilities on the trip, they had to interact with her. My wife knew that she was a problem but needed her. Volunteers were hard to find. She took what she could get.

Toward the end of the week, Fritz's shoes fell apart and Maria offered to take him to buy new shoes. Since I was the driver, I took them to town. In the shoe store, Fritz wandered around the store, looking at different pairs of shoes. He was going at his own pace, taking his time. Maria was impatient.

"I think he needs more time," I tried to tell her, hoping that she would understand me. Maybe she did, but she ignored me, and picked out a pair of shoes that she thought Fritz should buy. He tried them on, and from the expression on his face, it was clear to me that he didn't like them. He tried to put them back in the box.

"No, these are the right shoes," she insisted. "Come, let's go to the cashier so you can pay for them." I noticed that he was agitated and trying to resist her, but she took his wallet and paid for the shoes.

Maria then decided that the three of us should go get coffee and cake; it was mid-afternoon and it's a traditional thing to do. On the way, she handed me some postcards she had written. "Here, you mail these." She hadn't asked me. She had given me an order, at least it sounded that way to me. I thought to myself, does she think I have a disability, too? Does she think that she's my mother?

In a barely audible voice, I said, "You fucking bitch." I don't know if she understood what I said, but she must have heard the tone of my voice and seen the look on my face, because she told me off. I didn't understand what she actually said, but I got the message. In the middle of scolding me, I turned my back on her and walked away. That really pissed her off.

I was angry at her, but even more, I was shocked at myself: when I'm angry at a woman, I don't call her a "fucking bitch." I think that's unacceptable. I confront other men when they do that.

I walked around the block, trying to catch my breath, and calm myself. I wanted to challenge her for the way that she had treated Fritz, and I wanted to take him back to the store and support him in getting the shoes he wanted. I didn't want to piss her off. But I didn't have the words to say to Maria what I was thinking and feeling. All I had was the verbal ability of a three-year-old, and I had just had a temper tantrum.

That evening, with my wife's help as translator, I apologized to Maria. She didn't reciprocate. At least in this interaction with her, I behaved like an adult.

* * * * *

Unfortunately, my experience with Maria was not an isolated event. There were other times that I felt angry and expressed myself inappropriately. A few months after the trip to northern Germany, my wife and I were in our old apartment in Nürnberg. It was too small and we had decided to move. But we had to paint it. It was owned by a company that had lots of apartments like this, and there were official procedures that we had to follow before we could terminate the lease. I had spent several days painting the apartment, getting it ready for the inspection.

I am a good painter. My first real job as a teenager was working for Tommy Doyle, a painting contractor in northern New Jersey. I worked for him for about five years, during every summer vacation and holiday. Tommy taught me lots of tricks, and I was an eager student.

So painting this apartment was easy for me, and I thought I had done a good job. The apartment was old, and the surfaces were showing their age, but everything had a new coat of paint. I think it looked pretty good, given it was a simple, cheap apartment.

The inspector had a different opinion. According to him, I had made two big mistakes. I painted the doors off white instead of pure white. I thought it would look better; in the U.S., we always did that because the dirt doesn't show as much, and yet it still looks white. Instead of removing the special wallpaper they use here—which is meant to be painted and was already painted when my wife first moved into the apartment—I simply added another coat of white. If I had removed the paper, it would have exposed the bare plaster and would have looked worse. At least that was my opinion.

According to him, the apartment was unacceptable. We would have to pay to have the wallpaper removed and the doors repainted by one of the painters on their approved list. I was furious but unable to express my thoughts and feelings in German. I was not able to tell him why I thought I was right and he was wrong. I couldn't communicate my anger at a system that I didn't understand.

In contrast, my wife had a polite conversation with him and tried to explain our position. He was still unwilling to change his opinion, at which point I lost my temper and swore at him in English. I suspect he understood. My wife was stunned. She had never seen me like this. Not surprisingly, he got more rigid the angrier I got. We now had a male pissing contest, and my wife was in the middle.

Of course we lost the argument, and of course we had to pay for someone else to do the work.

I don't think I would have behaved this way in the U.S. I could have remained cool and firm. I could have expressed my thoughts. I could have communicated with my wife so we could decide together what to do. I could have understood that he was only doing his job and following the rules laid down by the company and even empathized with the position he is in. Maybe we could have negotiated something.

A few days later, after I had calmed down and accepted the situation, I wrote in my journal, "What is this anger? Is this something about culture shock? Is it something about the arrogance and entitlement I carry with me as a citizen of the U.S.? Is this something about my being a man, and my potential for aggression, and trying to take on the world, forgetting that there are women like my wife who are better able to deal with this than I am? Am I simply an angry person? What is wrong with me?"

A couple of years later, as I was searching for materials on learning a second language, I came across a book called *Lost in Translation* by Eva Hoffman. It was the first book I had found in which someone described the pain of learning a second language. I couldn't put the book down, and re-read it as soon as I was finished.

Hoffman's experience was different from mine—she moved from Poland to North America when she was a child—but there were so many things in her book that resonated with my experience. She described what I was feeling but not yet able to put into words.

> Linguistic dispossession is a sufficient motive for violence, for it is close to the dispossession of one's self. Blind, helpless rage is a rage that has no words—rage that overwhelms one with darkness. If one is perpetually without words, if one exists in the entropy of inarticulateness, that condition is bound to be an enraging frustration. …. Anger can be borne—it can even be satisfying—if it can gather into words and explore in a storm, or a rapier-sharp attack. But without this means of ventilation, it only turns back inward, building and swirling like a head of steam—building to an impotent, murderous rage. (p. 124)

Like Hoffman, the anger I sometimes experienced in Germany felt primal, as if my survival was at stake. I didn't want to kill anyone. But there were moments that I felt intense anger at native German speakers who couldn't, or didn't want to, understand me and treat me as an equal.

Of course, there were situations when I didn't get angry, when people were friendly and generous with me. But even though I had many "good experiences," the "bad" ones had a stronger and longer lasting impact. So, it was easy for me to reach the conclusion that I was unwelcome here.

I knew from my work in the U.S. that anger is a powerful feeling that cannot simply be ignored. So, if I didn't recognize and begin to deal with the anger I felt, I knew that it would eat at me and destroy my relationships with others, and other people would be hurt. I also knew that it was not easy to suddenly change my feelings and how I expressed them especially when I felt so unsure of my place here and was not able to find my voice.

* * * * *

As I observed my anger, it seemed that I had more anger here than I did in the U.S. It's not that I wasn't angry in the U.S. I was. I was angry at many things, and expressed that anger through writing and political activity, and by confronting people, sometimes gently, sometimes not. What was different here was I didn't have a way to express my anger in German or protect myself when faced with situations that felt threatening. That made it worse. I couldn't find an adult voice when I was angry. I only had the gestures and voice of a child. It was exactly what Eva Hoffman described.

I felt this rage again one day when I was riding my bike in Nürnberg: a dog on a leash lunged at me and nipped me on the leg. It was nothing more than a nick of my skin, but it happened so quickly that I was stunned. I kicked the dog, and it backed off.

The owner looked shocked that I had kicked her dog. She apologized, telling me that the dog was sick and not usually like that. Then I got more aggressive: I told her, in awkward German but with a very hostile tone of voice, "If your dog does that again, it's dead." She looked scared and backed off.

An hour later, I was still shaking from the incident. But enough time had passed that I was beginning to think about what had happened. I asked myself, who was more threatening? Her dog or me?

And then there was an incident with a German driver. One night, as I was crossing a street in the old part of the city, a big silver Mercedes almost hit me. I gave the driver a threatening look, he ignored it, and so I tapped on the passenger window to get his attention. I wanted to confront him. He gestured with his hand, a gesture I understood as, "Go away, I can't be bothered with you. So I became more aggressive, and slapped my open palm twice on the passenger side door.

That got his attention. He stepped out of his car.

I now had a better look at him. He was a grey haired man, about my age and size, dressed in a dark suit and topcoat. He approached and said, "I'm going to call the police because you hit my car."

I thought to myself, he's got to be kidding. There was no damage to his car, maybe some bruising on my hand. I later learned that some Germans, especially men, treat their car as the most important thing in their lives, more important than their wives and children.

"What? You almost hit me!," I told him, in German, with anger in my voice.

"That doesn't interest me," he replied, and pulled out his cell phone, presumably to call the police.

I was both scared and angry, and aware that I couldn't find the words I wanted in German. The thought occurred to me to switch to English. I suddenly didn't care if he understood me or not. It was important for me to find my voice and not let him intimidate me.

So I told him, in English, "My life is more important than your car."

He pointed his finger at me, and with a stern and patronizing tone, replied in English, "You're in Germany now, not in England, and you can't act like that here. Go back where you came from."

I didn't respond, and walked away. He got back in his car and drove off.

I was both surprised and not surprised by his behavior and my response. I had seen men like him do the same thing in the U.S., sometimes more aggressively. I had also responded in similar ways in the U.S., for example, when I was jogging and was almost hit by a car. So, I knew about my own capacity to be aggressive.

In this situation, I was being petty and hostile with him and could have gotten myself in trouble. As a foreigner here, I am at greater risk for getting in trouble than he is, but I think I was even more stunned by his comment to me that I should leave his country.

This was not the first time, nor would it be the last time, that a German man confronted me for violating a traffic law. For reasons I still don't understand, violations of traffic laws seem to be one of the few circumstances in which German men directly confront people who they think are doing something wrong. In this case, however, I was actually doing nothing wrong. I was in the crosswalk, inside the lines, and the driver of the silver Mercedes went through the crosswalk.

However, this was the first time that I had personally experienced German hostility to foreigners, and I began to realize that the anger I was feeling was not simply due to "linguistic dispossession." It was also a result of my status as a foreigner in Germany. The hostility from the driver of the silver Mercedes was mild in comparison to the treatment of immigrants who don't look like they are German or western European. They are routinely stopped by police who check their passports. They are treated rudely in city offices. They have been assaulted and even murdered because of their skin color and appearance as foreigners.

In contrast, I didn't even carry my passport. No one ever checked me to see if I had a right to be where I was. I got treated relatively well. I didn't fear being physically attacked because I am an immigrant. My identity as a U.S. citizen protected me—not from being ignored or mistreated on occasion—but from being threatened and attacked.

In fact, because I am a privileged white person with a U.S. passport, my security here was pretty much guaranteed. I was not going to get deported, but if I were someone without official permission to be in Germany, someone from one of the former Yugoslavian states, or an African nation, or the Middle East, I might get picked up in the middle of the night and deported. That has happened.

Even though they hold German passports, my friends Matho from India and Francois from the Democratic Republic of the Congo have had to learn how to be very diplomatic so that they can survive here. They are very cautious about expressing the anger they feel as immigrants. I didn't need to learn how to be cautious, because I was treated as a "good" immigrant. I had more freedom to express my anger without risk of punishment.

I rarely heard negative comments about people like me from the U.S. In contrast, I heard Germans make comments about other immigrants in ways that sometimes left me speechless.

For example, in the local newspaper I often saw the expression *farbige Leute* (colored people). When I read that, I thought I was back in the U.S. in the 1950's. Then I heard the word *Neger*, and it sounded exactly like *nigger* to me. A neighbor, whom I considered a friend and who had worked internationally, told me one day, "*Neger* babies are cute." A woman I met at a party, who has a University degree, laughingly told me, "There must have been a *neger* involved" when I made a comment about her daughter's curly hair. An acquaintance, who

— *49* —

is a manager in a company and married to a brown-skinned woman from South America, said to me, "Cooper, have you been in the sun? You are tanned like a *neger*."

In each of these cases, I believe that the people who made the comments were well intentioned and using what they thought was completely acceptable language. I know it isn't fair to apply U.S. standards to Germany, and just because a word sounds "bad" to me, it doesn't mean that it is "bad" in German. However, there are a few Germans who see this the same way I do and who think carefully about the language they use to talk about racial identity. A man who works with immigrants in a social service organization, who knew about my work in the U.S., asked me if I thought *neger* was an acceptable word to use. There is a group called Der Braune Mob (the Brown Mob) who explain on their web site why the words *Neger* and *farbige* are unacceptable.

Then there were incidents when Germans shared their prejudices about immigrants directly with me. The first time I experienced this was in 2004 at a ceremony honoring the work my wife had done with people with disabilities. She wanted me to be there, and I wasn't sure if I wanted to go. I didn't know if I would be able to communicate with her colleagues and if they would be patient with my attempts to speak German. However, I wanted to support her, so I decided to go.

My wife introduced me to one of her colleagues who was also a social worker. I was not sure exactly what she did, but because of her training as a social worker I assumed that she would be a compassionate and understanding type of person. After exchanging names, I apologized for how bad my German was.

"Oh no," she said in response, "your German is good. But the Turkish people—they don't know how to speak German, and they don't want to learn German."

I was astounded to hear this from a complete stranger within minutes of having met me. I thought we would be making small talk. I was reminded of times in the U.S. when white people who didn't know me very well would tell me how awful Black people are, as if as they automatically expected me to share their opinion.

I didn't agree with her assessment of Turkish people, and I took her prejudice personally. I could easily have been one of those immigrants she was describing. I didn't speak German very well, and even though I was trying to learn, there were times when I didn't want to learn this language.

I tried to tell her about my experience learning German, how difficult it was and my lack of desire to speak German, but I was unable to explain myself, either because my German was not good enough or she wasn't interested in listening to me. Even if I could have described my experience, I doubt it would have made any impact on her prejudice. There is lots support for her position: some prominent Germans think exactly the same way, and the government treats different immigrants differently. There is a hierarchy of worth: some immigrants are considered better than others.

Of course this hierarchy has an impact on motivation to learn the language. I happen to belong to one of those groups that is considered better, and so my efforts get noticed and appreciated. It reminds me of well known research about education: if teachers expect you to succeed, you have a better chance of succeeding.

The prejudice expressed by my wife's colleague is not unique to Germany. I heard the same kind of comments in the U.S.: complaints about Latin Americans who speak Spanish on the job, complaints about the accents of salespeople or employees at call centers in Asia, complaints about young immigrants who create their own version of English.

Because of my work challenging oppression, I felt a responsibility to respond when I heard these kinds of comments in the U.S. Of course, there were many times I didn't respond because of the situation, because I was dealing with something else, or because I just didn't have the energy. But when I did respond, I had options for how I could express my thoughts and feelings.

Here, I felt impotent. I didn't understand the context, and I didn't have the words to respond.

My experience with my wife's colleague would not be my last opportunity to confront Germans on their prejudice toward Turkish people. People living in and around Nürnberg would give me other opportunities to practice. Eventually I would be able to confront them and tell them about the experience of being an immigrant. And I would be able to do it with respect for the other person, and not as if I were having a temper tantrum.

Sadness

In the textbooks and study guides we used in Grundstufe 2 and 3, there were stories and pictures about white skinned Germans of all ages and from different regions of Germany, engaged in typically German activities. There were no stories and pictures about foreigners living in Germany. Nor were there stories about Black Germans: people of African ancestry who were born in Germany and had German passports. Nor were there stories about immigrants who had become German citizens, or their children and grandchildren, many of whom considered themselves to be German, or at least hyphenated German.

I guess that the curriculum was designed to teach us about mainstream German culture, or at least what the textbook writers believe is mainstream. If that's true, then it reflected the dominant German perspective on integration: that we immigrants should assimilate.

And yet, even immigrants who had assimilated, who spoke perfect German and had German passes, weren't necessarily considered German. Native Germans frequently asked them, "Where do you come from?" If the answer were Stuttgart or Hamburg, the response might be, "No, I mean, where do you really come from?"

In Grundstufe 4, the textbooks we used came from a different publisher. There were a few lessons that included stories and pictures of immigrants, albeit "successful" immigrants. There was even a lesson on the various types of legal status that a foreigner might have. One teacher used class time to explain the law and then facilitated a discussion in the class about our own stories of immigration and citizenship. I really appreciated that he did that. But most of time, I didn't see my life, or the lives of other immigrants, reflected in my German lessons.

I wish that the curriculum had been based on our experiences living in Germany, and asked us questions like "Who are you? Why are you here? What are you feeling and thinking about your life here?" For some students and teachers, these questions might be too personal and seemingly not related to the task of learning German, but for me, and maybe others, it would have been exactly what we needed.

And if some of us had wanted these kinds of discussions, I don't know how much German fluency we would have needed before we could answer these questions. I am sure that there is a way that a curriculum could be built around these questions, even for beginners. It would have helped us remember who we are, and maybe find a new identity, as we struggled to find a new life in Germany.

I decided to start a support group for immigrants like myself. I had facilitated support groups in the U.S. and thought that I could do the same thing here. I found an organization willing to give me space on Friday nights to meet. I didn't know where to find the people to create a group, but I believed that there was a need for a group like this. I heard the voice that Kevin Costner heard in the film *Field of Dreams*: "Build it and they will come."

They came. They were Italian, Turkish, Venezuelan, Spanish, Brazilian, British, Vietnamese, Canadian, Romanian, Czech, and Russian. All of them trying to create a life for themselves in Nürnberg, and all of them trying to learn German. But because we were all beginners in German, we mostly used English in the group. It was the one common language we all had, even though our abilities to speak English varied.

One of the dominant themes of our conversations was our sadness about becoming "nobody" in Germany. We each had the sense that we were "somebody" in our home country. We had had family and friends, a job or career that gave us a sense of value. We lost that when we came here. We were not seen for who we were. Members of the support group described applying for jobs and hearing no response; trying to volunteer with an organization and being told that there was nothing available; knocking on neighbors' doors and trying to start conversations but not being invited into their homes.

One woman talked about her sadness of not being greeted by strangers. She enjoyed running, and missed the experience of saying "hi" and exchanging smiles with perfect strangers when she was out for a run in her home country. She also played on a soccer team in Nürnberg, and one night wanted to share her good news that she had finally gotten a full time job. Instead of congratulating her, as she expected, the women on her team wondered if she would continue to play on the team. She realized it could have been an indirect way to tell her that they liked her, but she wanted a more direct and clear expression of their support.

We all felt some degree of social coldness as we interacted with Germans living in Nürnberg, in spite of the fact that we were trying to adjust to being here. Several of the people who attended the group were very clear that they wanted to leave Germany because they didn't feel that they were welcomed here.

It might sound like we were whining a little bit. After all, we had chosen to live here. An older Russian Jewish woman—who I liked, and who liked me—confronted me one night, telling me, "You're not a real immigrant. You have a choice about where you live. You can leave." She didn't believe she had options about where she could live.

She was right. I am a privileged immigrant. Nonetheless, the pain I felt was real, and I was not used to being treated as an outsider. I suspect that less privileged immigrants have thicker skin, or worse, have internalized the sense that they are "less than."

The support group was a good idea, but it also turned out to be more work than I wanted. In hindsight, I was not ready to be the facilitator. I needed the group for my own support. It was too hard to be in both roles.

* * * * *

Sometimes I was invisible here. That was astounding to me. I couldn't recall ever feeling that way in my life, certainly not as an adult. Like the people in the support group, I thought I was "somebody" in the U.S. and here I seemed to be "nobody."

My wife and I went to the bank to get some information about my account. I asked the bank officer questions, using my basic classroom German, and he gave his answers to my wife. He didn't look at me once. The same thing happened in stores when we were shopping together and at city agencies when we had to deal with some aspect of my legal status in Germany.

There was not much I could do. I didn't have the verbal skills to participate in these conversations. So I observed what happened and complained about it later to my wife.

Unfortunately sometimes I took out my frustration on her and blamed her for not including me in the conversation. But this was not her fault. I think the anger came in part from my feeling dependent on her. I couldn't do things here that I could do by myself in the U.S.

Being dependent was not the image I had of myself. In the U.S., I thought of myself as independent. It actually wasn't true—my life was dependent on a vast network of people who provided food, clothing, transportation, employment, emotional support, even love—but the culture in the U.S. encourages a myth of independence and individualism. I am a product of this myth and have bought into it.

I hadn't yet realized how dependent on other people I actually am and always have been. I hadn't yet realized that my relationship with my wife and my life in Germany was an opportunity for me to learn how things really are in life. I hadn't yet realized that my being dependent on her and her on me is an aspect of intimacy in a relationship.

After trying to blame her a few times and seeing that it didn't help, I was able to tell her that I simply wanted to be included in the conversation. We agreed that the next time this happened she would try to include me, and I would be assertive and speak up even if I were being ignored.

We soon had an opportunity to try our new strategy. Our kitchen stove stopped working, so we went shopping for a new one. The salesman ignored me and explained all the technical aspects to my wife. She told him, "I don't understand much about stoves and besides, my husband is the one who does all the cooking." Then, turning to me, she said, "Cooper, what do you think about this stove?" The salesman still ignored me.

I tried a different strategy. I know some technical things about appliances, and so I tried to make some "guy talk" with him about one of electronic features he showed us. He barely responded to me and instead explained a different feature to my wife. So the "male bonding" approach didn't work either.

Part of me was thinking, this guy is stupid. Does he want this sale or not? And I was also getting a little pissed off at him.

Despite his behavior, we were considering buying a stove from him, because there was one that had the features we wanted. Now we had to talk about the price. He offered us what he thought was a great deal and then proceeded to pressure us to sign a contract. I don't like being pressured. Now he had pushed me over the edge. In the best German I could muster—I practiced the lines in my head before I delivered them—I sarcastically told him, "My friend, you are just a salesman, trying to get us to buy this. Do you think we're stupid? We are not going to buy anything here."

My wife looked a little shocked. Not only had I been sarcastic instead of polite, as she would have been, I had used the informal form of *you*, which a native German speaker would probably never do with a salesman in this situation.

I violated a cultural rule. But my wife was also proud of me, and a bit envious that I confronted him. She would have liked to confront him, but didn't feel like she could or should. She has been conditioned to be nice and avoid conflict.

We walked out and went to another store. We bought a stove from a salesman who talked to both of us.

I liked the new stove. I enjoy cooking, and I think I'm a good cook. I do almost all of the cooking for us. In the first couple of years that I was here, it was a way for me to feel some sense of self-worth. If people came for dinner to our house, and if I cooked for them, maybe I would get some attention, instead of being ignored.

But I was disappointed.

My wife invited a former colleague to dinner. She brought her husband. I asked him some questions, he answered my wife. The amazing part is that he was an English teacher. Here I was, trying my best to use German—I didn't use English that evening, and neither did he—and he seemed completely insensitive to my situation.

On another occasion, I asked one of my German teachers to dinner, and she talked almost the whole time with my wife, using the local Nürnberg dialect. My wife understood this dialect, but I didn't. Another couple came to visit. She spoke clearly, asked me questions, and listened to me, but I couldn't understand what her boyfriend was saying. I asked him several times to slow down, and for good measure, explained why, wanting to reassure him that it was not his fault. It had no impact on him. After they left, my wife told me that he spoke like someone reading a paper in a lecture, as if he were trying to impress us. He used big words and long, complicated sentences. No wonder I didn't understand.

Stephanie, one of my wife's former colleagues, came to our apartment one night, and the three of us played a popular board game called *Siedler*. Stephanie explained the rules to me. I didn't really understand. She spoke quickly and didn't check with me to see if I was following her. But I learn by doing things, so I suggested that we start playing rather than asking her to repeat what I probably wouldn't understand.

I was losing badly, and she was not helping me or making allowances for me. When I am in her position, teaching someone a game, I give them suggestions, I encourage them to take back a move and make a better choice, sometimes I intentionally lose so that they can win. If this were golf, I would give them a handicap.

But she was doing none of that. Instead, she seemed to be enjoying the fact that she was winning. I felt a sense of resignation. It wasn't fun.

The irony was that Stephanie worked with people with disabilities. According to my wife, she was good at it. Later, I asked my wife, "Why was Stephanie so competitive and insensitive with me? Didn't she realize that I was at a real disadvantage using German?" My wife couldn't give me an answer, and I didn't try to play *Siedler* again for a long time.

At first, when people treated me like this, my wife didn't notice it. But after I pointed it out several times, she was shocked at how often it happened. What I really appreciated is that she noticed it. If she had discounted my experience in some way, I would have felt really hurt.

I cooked some great meals for our guests, and didn't get much in return for my effort, except for a couple of insights. In my good moments, when I was feeling relatively secure, I sat back and observed what was happening. I realized that my experience of invisibility might be unusual for me as a relatively privileged man. I had heard women talk about how frequently this happens to them when they are with groups of men. The men ignore them, while the women play the role of asking questions to keep the conversation going.

I got used to being ignored and was no longer surprised when it happened. But sometimes there were lingering questions: is something wrong with me? Do native German speakers think it isn't worth their time talking with me? I tried to remember that there was probably another explanation for their behavior: that they were uncomfortable communicating with me because my German was not very good. Maybe they were afraid that they wouldn't understand me, or that I wouldn't understand them. Maybe they simply didn't know how to communicate with someone who was at a beginner level in German. Maybe their behavior said something about them, and not about me.

And then there are moments when it turned out a little differently, when native German speakers realized the impact of their behavior on me. I met a woman at a talk one night. We got together a couple of times for coffee and really enjoyed our time together. Then she came to dinner at our place, met my wife and had a great conversation with her. But I was largely left out of it, and while she had used standard German with me, she and my wife spoke dialect. The next time I saw her, I told her what I had felt, and she apologized to me. After that, she always used standard German if I was a part of the conversation.

There were also a couple of men, friends of my wife, who came to our house alone or with partners. They didn't ignore me, but after a year or two of occasional social contact, and an improvement in my German, they each admitted that they were surprised that I had something interesting to say. They had always complimented my cooking, but that's about all they had seen in me.

In one way, I can understand this. My level of German made it difficult for me to participate in adult conversations. I probably sounded like a five-year-old discussing adult topics. If I grew tired, I would stop talking because my German deteriorated.

However, the implication of what the two men said is a bit painful: immigrants who don't speak German very well are less worthy of contact. I have seen native English speakers behave this way toward immigrants in the U.S. So, I knew it was a possibility that native German speakers do the same thing here.

* * * * *

On one of my first trips back to the U.S., I ran into an acquaintance who had lived in Germany and spoke German. I told him how hard it was for me to be in Germany.

Before moving to Germany, I had been very critical of the U.S. But now that I was living in Germany, I had suddenly become a defender of the U.S. and very critical of Germans and German culture. I couldn't see much that was positive about living in Germany.

I couldn't see much that was positive about German as a language, either. I told him that German sounded harsh, the words were long and incomprehensible, the grammar was too complicated, and the dialects I heard didn't sound anything like the German I was learning.

He told me, "Judging the culture and people is a predictable phase of culture shock. I suggest that you avoid comparing the two cultures, and avoid comparing the two languages. Just notice the differences, and notice how you communicate in each language." It was wise advice.

The idea of accepting differences as they are, without judging, wasn't a new concept for me. I had used this principle in my work on multiculturalism and diversity, and I had learned through meditation the skill of seeing and accepting things as they are. Nonetheless, I needed to be reminded.

Deciding to accept German culture, as it is, was one of the decisions I needed to make if I were to find some degree of happiness in Germany. I eventually was able to do that, more or less, but it took time, and practice, and still there were periods when I became very judgmental of German culture and German people.

And after being here a few years, I realized that my conclusion, "Germans don't want to make contact with immigrants" was an exaggeration and generalization, and said as much about my feelings as it did about the behavior of Germans. There are Germans who clearly don't want anything to do with immigrants, but there are also Germans who welcome or at least accept our presence. They "make contact" with us in a way that is different from what I expect or want.

So, for the most part I stopped saying, "Germans are unfriendly." Instead, I tried to use words that I had heard Germans themselves using to describe their culture, like "private", "holding back," "formal," and "a little nervous or unsure of how to make contact with foreigners." Still, in a moment of frustration or as an expression of solidarity with other immigrants, I would occasionally slip and say, "Germans are unfriendly." It wasn't fair, but it was a way to express my feelings.

* * * * *

One day I met a woman from the U.S. who had been living in Germany for about ten years. She told me, "I can't be myself in German. I'm funny when I speak English, but I'm not funny in German. If I can't express my humor, then I'm not expressing my sense of myself."

In the support group I started, there were times that people were unable to express their thoughts and feelings because of their limited ability in a second language. There was an Italian woman who spoke German with us because she didn't feel confident enough to use English. Her German wasn't great, but we understood what she was saying, or at least we thought we did. One evening, she wanted to talk about a painful experience she had recently had. She was having a hard time expressing her feelings in German. We encouraged her to switch to Italian.

At first she resisted, saying that we wouldn't understand her. But we gently encouraged her, and when she finally started speaking Italian, she became a different person. We didn't understand the words she was telling us, but we understood her feelings. Afterwards she told us that she had found the emotional release she needed.

On another evening, we encouraged a man from Venezuela to use Spanish. English was difficult for him; when he spoke Spanish, his eyes became bright and a smile appeared on his face. A Polish woman sounded sexy and playful when she spoke Polish but formal and serious when she spoke German or English.

I noticed something similar when I attended a seminar in France with participants from several European countries. Our working language was English, but there were also situations where we were interacting with native French speakers in the community.

One of the participants, a Romania man, sounded very different depending on the language he was using. When he spoke Romanian, he sounded relaxed; when he spoke French, in which he was fluent, he sounded excited; and when he spoke English, he sounded rigid. His English ability was much lower than his French.

As I carefully listened to him speak English, I realized he often used the verbs *should* and *must* in combination with another verb, as in, "You must listen to this," or "I should know that." It gave his English an authoritarian quality. It was easy to imagine him having an authoritarian personality. When he spoke French or Romanian, on the other hand, he seemed to be a different person: playful and loving.

There was also an Italian woman at the conference who was an English teacher. We got to talking about second language use, and I mentioned to her what I had noticed with the Romanian man. "I think that's common," she said, "when people are learning to use a second language. They depend on 'helping verbs' because you can use them with the infinitive form of a verb, and you don't need to be able to conjugate that verb. You just need to know how to conjugate the helping verb, and you usually learn about 'helping verbs' in the beginning stages of a new language. Learning how to conjugate all the other verbs you need in a language takes a lot more time."

I realized that I did the same thing in German. I said things like, "Du musst das machen" (you have to do that), whereas in English I might say, "I think it would a good idea to do that," or "it's pretty important that you do that," or "if I were in your position, I might do that." The German version sounded too direct, almost aggressive. The English versions sounded indirect and softer, but I didn't know how to do that in German.

I also said some things in German that simply didn't make sense, or sounded ridiculous, in a particular social context. I thought I had clearly communicated what I wanted to say, but native German speakers looked puzzled, or took offense, at what I had said.

My German teacher in Boston—the man who first gave me lessons—taught me some words and phrases that were fun to say but not very useful, like *Jakobs muscheln* (scallops) or *ober Affen Titten geil* (literally, *over monkey breasts horny*, but translated as *really, really cool*).

When I got to Germany and tried using *ober Affen Titten geil* to express enthusiasm for something, my wife looked at me like I was crazy. Maybe teenagers used that expression ten years ago, but no adult would say that.

Something similar would happen occasionally with my wife. She learned English in school—formal British English, and she spent time in England. So, she has a bit of a British accent and sometimes uses expressions that sound foreign to me. Or she uses words that are technically correct but which don't make sense because the context is wrong. Or she makes up a word, based on what she thinks should make sense. Most of the time, though, she uses language that I understand.

If she says something that doesn't make sense to me, and if I'm in a good mood, I say, "I don't understand what you are trying to tell me. Could you repeat what you just said?" When that doesn't work, I ask her, "Could you say that in a different way? I really want to understand." It takes a little more time to have a conversation like this, but I like how the conversation feels. It brings me closer to her.

If, on the other hand, we are in the middle of a difficult conversation about our relationship, or if I am talking about something that is very important to me, I feel an urgency to be understood and to understand her. Instead of being patient, I sometimes get hurt or offended by what she says because I am simply reacting to her words.

I know that the last thing she wants to do is hurt my feelings or offend me, but I forget that. Instead, I get angry with her.

After a few years of living with her, I figured out another way to listen to her, not taking her words too literally, but listening to the feelings and thoughts she is trying to express. When I learned to do this, I avoided a lot of our miscommunications and occasional fights.

On the other hand, I often wondered what other people hear when I speak German. And based on what they hear, who do they think I am? And regardless of what native German speakers hear, who *am* I in this new language?

I didn't have answers to these questions, but when I later read some of the research on second language learning, I learned about a possible connection between identity and language. Some experts believe that our cultural identities affect our ability to learn a second language, and that our cultural identities change as we use a second language.

This resonates with my experience. My ability to use German depends on how others see me and how I see myself. The longer I am here and using German, the more I change. I am different from who I was when I first came here.

* * * * *

After being here three years, I began to call myself an immigrant. It was an attempt to say, "I live here, and I'm staying." It reminded me that I was making a choice to be here and that I did have choices about my life here.

I told Karuna, my first German teacher, about my new identity. She gave me a book that she thought might be interesting to me: *Zweiheimisch: Bikulturell Leben in Deutschland*. It is a collection of interviews with young immigrants who describe their bicultural life in Germany and have two homes: the country in which they grew up and Germany.

I hadn't really wanted to read anything in German because it was too overwhelming. I had read some children's books out loud to my nieces and nephews, but I hadn't read a "real" book written for adults. Although it took work and patience and although the voices are those of young people, I finished *Zweiheimisch* because it grabbed my attention. The young people described some of the things I was experiencing.

In German, there are several ways I can describe my identity and status. I can say, "I come from the United States but I live here." Or I can use one of the German words that describe people like me: an *Ausländer* (foreigner or foreign national), *Einwanderer* (immigrant), or maybe a *Fremder* (foreigner). *Migrant*, although it sounds like the English word *immigrant*, is used here to describe migrant workers.

None of the German words felt quite right. They didn't fit my sense of who I was. Nor did the English equivalents. I was not used to describing myself as a foreigner or immigrant. Telling people that I come from the U.S. sounded the best to me, but it avoided the issue of identity. So, I decided to use *Ausländer* in German and *immigrant* in English, at least some of the time. After another couple of years, I used *Immigrant* in German, and then later, "I have an immigrant background."

I mentioned my thoughts about this to several people from the U.S and England who also live here, and their reaction surprised me. They didn't like the word *immigrant*. They called themselves *ex-pats*, or simply said that they have been living here for a while, but they did not identify themselves as immigrants.

At first I didn't understand why they resisted the label *immigrant*. I was forgetting that many of them are middle class people working for a multinational corporation, and I was forgetting that our view of immigrants in the U.S. and England has not always been positive. Even though most of us in the U.S. are descended from immigrants, we probably don't identify with the immigrants welcomed by the Statue of Liberty: the tired, poor, homeless, wretched refuse, huddled masses yearning to breathe free.

And, I had to admit, that didn't exactly describe my status as an immigrant to Germany. I am a white man from the U.S. with a master's degree and a successful career behind him. I have some savings for retirement. I am trying to find my voice and identity in this strange country. I am not a traumatized refugee or asylum seeker. I am not poor or homeless.

Some people welcomed my presence here. I had a chance of succeeding. I had the luxury of claiming an identity as an immigrant even if it sounded a bit strange. My identity was changing.

Even so, I was not sure how I really felt about this. I was not ready to let go of my identity as "someone from the U.S."

* * * * *

In a novel by Rohinton Mistry, *A Fine Balance*, I read a passage that gave me some relief from the sadness I was feeling as I lived in Germany and tried to use this language. As he is reflecting on his life, Vasantrao Valmik says,

> How much have I lost? Ambition, solitude, words, eyesight, vocal cords. In fact, that is the central theme of my life story—loss. But isn't it the same with all life stories? Loss is essential. Loss is part and parcel of that necessary calamity called life.
>
> Mind you, I'm not complaining. Thanks to some inexplicable universal guiding force, it is always the worthless things we lose – slough off, like a moulting snake. Losing, losing again, is the very basis of the life process, till all we are left with is the bare essence of human existence. (page 555)

Like I did with the words of the young person in Liberia, I copied this and put it on the wall next to my desk. It helped me put my experience in context.

Rules

Like any language, German has many rules. There are rules for the order of words in a sentence, rules for conjugating verbs, rules for when and how to use prepositions, and rules for the endings of adjectives depending on the noun they modify. This is only a partial list. Of course, there are many exceptions to these rules.

For example, in German the article *the* changes depending on whether the noun is feminine, masculine, neutral, or plural. And it changes depending on its function in a sentence. Because of this, there are six different forms of the word *the*. I can't see that this adds anything to comprehension. It only increases opportunities to make mistakes and opportunities to be corrected.

Some of the problem is that German has kept a concept of case, which we no longer have in English. There are four cases in German: Nominativ, Akkusativ, Dativ, and Genitiv. It's sort of like the difference between a subject and an object in a sentence in English but more complicated.

One day after class, I asked my wife about case. She had no idea what I was referring to. Growing up with the language, she just learned how to deal with case but didn't learn, or can't remember, the rules about case. I asked other students, and they were puzzled, too, except a student from Russia. She understood the concept of case, and then told me that there are more cases in Russian than in German. Poor woman, I thought.

In one grammar book, I read that case is important: without it, the meaning of a word in a sentence is unclear. In my worst moments, I thought that the only reason for case in German was to make students like me suffer. Some teachers told us that we didn't have to bother learning Genitiv because its use is dying out. I wish the other cases would also die out.

Then there are the rules that cover the pronoun *you*. In German, there are three different forms of *you*: the informal singular *you* (*du*), the informal plural *you* (*ihr*), the formal *you* (*Sie*). At least, *Sie* is the same for both singular and plural, otherwise there would be four forms of *you*.

Moreover, each of these three forms of *you* takes a different verb. For some reason I don't understand, I first learned how to conjugate the *du* form of verbs, then the *Sie* form, and much later the *ihr* form. So, for a while I didn't know how to talk to the couple who lived across from us. If Marcus were by himself in the kitchen, I knew how to ask him, "What are you cooking?" But if he and his wife Claudia were cooking together, I didn't know how to ask them what *they* were cooking.

Eventually, I learned how to conjugate verbs for all three forms of *you*, but when to actually use the formal or informal form of *you* was another matter. That decision is based on another kind of rule: an unwritten cultural belief about the correct way to address someone. Not only did I have to learn the rules of German grammar, I had to learn rules about how to use the language in social settings.

For example, I might know someone personally, and if we have coffee together, just of the two of us, we would use *du*. But if the two of were in a meeting at work with colleagues, I might be expected to use *Sie* with him.

If I didn't know someone who is obviously older than I am, I would use *Sie* and have to wait for them to ask me to use *du*. If it were someone obviously younger, I could initiate using *du*, but some younger people might feel really uncomfortable with that. The culture tells them that they must use *Sie* with me.

When my wife and I moved to a new apartment in the fall of 2004 and met some of our new neighbors, I suggested that we use *du* right away. They seemed to accept that. Other Germans told me that they would not use *du* with their neighbors. Better to keep the relationship at a distance. If there's a conflict, it will easier to deal with it. In my experience, it's the opposite: it's easier to deal with a conflict if I have a relationship with someone.

This distinction between the informal you and the formal you made contact with Germans awkward for me. I didn't know it yet, because I couldn't hear it, but Germans sometimes avoid using any form of *you* because they don't know which form to use and don't feel comfortable asking. I suspected that there was also an unwritten cultural rule that went something like, "You have to figure this out indirectly because asking directly is too impolite."

One night my wife and I went to dinner at the apartment of Frau and Herr Müller, a couple in their 60's. My wife and Frau Müller knew each other through work and used Sie with each other. When we arrived, we shook hands with each of them, said "hello," and then proceeded to talk about their apartment. From my perspective, I hadn't actually been introduced to Frau and Herr Müller because neither my wife nor the Müllers told me their first names. They referred to me as Herr Thompson.

I felt uncomfortable. They had invited us to dinner in their home. I wanted to be friendly and informal. I wanted to use their first names, but I sensed that I was not supposed to have this information. Because they were older, I was supposed to wait for them to initiate the use of *du*. So, I used *Sie* and addressed them as Frau and Herr Müller.

My wife and I avoided inviting them to our place for dinner. We thought we should—it seemed like the polite thing to do—and we had suggested it as we left their apartment. But we couldn't get very excited about spending time with them. It felt too awkward.

*****

Then there is a rule that immigrants must learn German, but this rule doesn't apply to all immigrants. It depends on what country you come from and why you are here. If you are considered a valuable employee or have an expertise that is needed here, then it's okay if you don't speak German. But if you are an "ordinary" immigrant, then you are expected to speak German, and criticized if you don't.

As a citizen of the U.S., I am not really expected to learn German. I have almost never heard any criticism of my people for not speaking German. Many of them don't. They just continue to use English and expect Germans to speak English with them. A former U.S. soldier, now married to a German woman and living here, told me, "I don't speak a word of German, and I have no intention of learning any."

I believe that it is important for immigrants to learn German, and the vast majority do. Some even learn to speak German on their own without attending classes. I wish that there would be some public recognition, even appreciation, that so many immigrants have learned German. In the time I have lived here, I have seldom heard native German speakers appreciate this fact although I have heard criticism of immigrants who don't learn German, as if there were a lot of them. I have seldom heard native Germans recognize that their country didn't want immigrants who came several decades ago as guest workers to learn German; it was expected that they would leave after putting in a few years building the German economy. Yet, some of these same immigrants are criticized now for not having learned German and for having spoken their native language at home to the detriment of their children's and grandchildren's education.

I also wish that there would be some understanding and empathy for people who have a lot of difficulty learning German. Some immigrants, especially older ones, attend classes but end up frustrated or depressed, because it is simply too difficult to learn another language or because the class is not designed for their needs. I don't believe it's fair to criticize them or simply require them to take more classes. It won't help them learn German. In his book, *Second Language Acquisition*, Rod Ellis writes, "It is one thing to learn a language when you respect and are respected by native speakers of that language. It is entirely different when you experience hostility from native speakers or when you wish to distance yourself from them." (p. 5)

Despite my own emotional resistance to learning German and despite the "permission" I had to keep speaking English, I believed that I should speak German when I was with native German speakers. There was one exception: I spoke English with my wife. It is the language we used when we met, and I had no desire to feel like I was a student when I was with her. This was fine with her, and she had never expected me to speak German with her. Over time, I met many other immigrants who also spoke German in public and their native language at home.

Using German in public seemed like the right thing for me to do. I was living here, and I thought I should use the language. The problem was, I was putting pressure on myself to use a language that I could barely use.

Nonetheless, my "German only" rule gave me lots of opportunities to practice. When I went to parties, or lectures, or stores, I always used German. Now and then my speaking partner shifted to English, but I almost always continued using German. My rule wouldn't allow me to switch, and I was firm about this. So, when Germans tried to use English with me, it didn't last very long. They soon switched back to German.

Occasionally I attended an English-speaking *stammtisch*—a group that regularly meets in a restaurant just to get together with other English speakers. I was surprised to hear others use English with the waiter when they ordered food and drinks. I wouldn't have thought of doing that. A few said that they were scared to use German. I understood their fear, and some part of me was envious that they had given themselves permission to use English.

At the same time, I didn't want to use English because then I might look like a typical American, many of whom come here and expect Germans to speak English with them. I felt embarrassed when my fellow citizens did that. Being associated with them was worse for me than whatever fear I might have had of using German.

Other native English speakers told me that it was hard for them to find native German speakers with whom they could practice German. They always switch to English when they realize that I'm a native English speaker. That prompted me to ask, "Why don't you just keep speaking German in spite of them?"

"It's easier to switch to English," they said.

I understood. It would have been easier for me, too, to use English, but the rule I had created for myself wouldn't let me do that.

Sometimes in the middle of a conversation with native speaking Germans I was confronted with another cultural rule: One should speak perfect German. Speaking grammatically correct German seemed to be a cultural rule that matters to people who attended a university. At least, they are the ones who tried to enforce this rule with me. Now and again someone, even a complete stranger, would suddenly correct a mistake I had made—maybe I had used the wrong ending on an adjective or the wrong form of a verb tense.

I don't like to be corrected when I haven't asked for it or if the person who wants to correct me hasn't asked my permission to do so. Even though I'm sure it is well intentioned, I experience this desire or need to correct me as condescending. I didn't ask these people to teach me. Instead of listening to me, they interrupted me. My grammar seemed more important to them than my thoughts or feelings. It reminded me of my father, and I didn't like it when he did it.

In contrast, I have never had a working class person or someone from the country correct me. No one in my wife's family has ever done this. They are interested in what I have to say and do their best to understand me. If I ask for a word or the correct form of something, then they help me. This kind of help I appreciate, and I am grateful that they have accepted the way I speak and accept me as I am instead of trying to teach me something.

After I had been here a few years, I developed some strategies to deal with this. One day I was on a train from Duisberg back to Nürnberg. I had been using only German for two days, and I had gotten compliments on my ability to communicate complex ideas in German.

I was sitting by myself on the train when a German man sat down next to me. We started a conversation, in German. I learned that he lives in Taiwan and speaks Chinese. I asked him about his experience of learning Chinese, and I told him a little bit about my experience learning German. A couple of times he corrected mistakes in my grammar. I noticed it, ignored him, and kept on talking.

Then he said, "Speaking perfect Chinese is important to me. It's a difficult language, but I study and practice a lot and ask native speakers to correct my mistakes." He must have noticed that I didn't clean up my mistakes after he corrected me.

"Speaking perfect German is not my goal," I told him. "I know I make mistakes, but it doesn't matter to me. I only want to communicate with people."

"But it's important to speak correctly."

"Not for me."

"But how will you learn the right way to speak German?"

"There's two things," I answered. "First, Germany is a country where being perfect and following rules are important. I come from a country where that is not as important. Of course, we have rules and laws, but I think there is also more freedom to make mistakes and make your own rules."

"I think you're right. I lived in the U.S. for a few years, and Germany is a country where order is very important."

"And second," I continued, "I do want people to help me with German, but only when I ask them or if they ask me for permission to correct me."

He paused. This was a new concept for him. "So, can I correct your mistakes?"

I smiled. "Yes, of course, because we had this conversation. Now it's okay."

Still, what struck me was his need to correct me. I guess it was not enough for him that we were simply two strangers having a conversation during a two hour train ride. I wanted to have a conversation; he wanted to be my teacher. I wanted to see us as equals despite my language deficit; if he decided on his own that it was his job to correct my mistakes, then it would feel to me like we were unequal. I didn't want that.

I asked my friend Francois about his experience with this—he was born in the Democratic Republic of Congo and has lived in Germany for over twenty years—and he told me, "Where I come from, if you don't know the local language, then you only need to learn what you need for your job or whatever you are doing there. That might be only a few words to use in the market."

"Here, if you are a taxi driver, the only German you really need is to understand directions and make small talk with customers. You don't need to learn German as if you are attending a university, but Germans expect you to speak a high level of German, even if you are a taxi driver. That means that immigrants are excluded from fully participating in this society."

"And," he added, "I think it's harder to learn German in Germany. If you went to the Congo and wanted to learn one of the languages that we speak, you could learn it faster because people want to speak with you. They don't correct your mistakes, they are just excited that you want to speak their language. Here, people generally aren't excited to speak with you or even excited that you want to learn their language."

Fortunately, I was not looking for a job here, so I didn't have to worry about Germans judging my ability to do a job based on my ability to speak German. But I did feel the pressure to speak in a way that Germans wanted me to speak. My task was to decide the level of German that I needed here, and to decide how I wanted to speak, instead of letting some Germans decide that for me. I needed to determine my own rules for using German.

* * * * *

My father and mother were my first language teachers. They both believed in the power of words. They both believed that there were right and wrong ways to use language. They had their own rules for how to speak.

Like all children, I accepted some of their beliefs as if they were truths. This happened unconsciously. Even if I had had my own beliefs about language, I didn't have the power to challenge them nor the freedom to find my own way with language.

As an adult, I am not always aware that I am following my parents' rules or that I have a choice about creating my own rules. I sometimes follow these rules blindly as if I were a child and had no choice in the matter. So, I am not surprised that these rules are still floating around in my head and that they impact my ability to learn German—like when I didn't know the word *Fahrstuhl* and thought that I would get in trouble for not understanding.

My mom emphasized being friendly and polite, not interrupting people or wasting their time, and always saying "please" and "thank you." My dad emphasized using correct grammar, and he loved to demonstrate how intelligent he thought he was by using obscure words and making a statement about any topic presented to him. He never said, "I don't know" or acted like he didn't understand. He expected the same of me.

Imagine that I am at Frau and Herr Müller's apartment. We are using formal German, and they speak very precisely. Right from the beginning, I feel nervous because I wonder what they will think of me, as I try to use my version of German, which is often incorrect.

They start to tell me about something. To show them that I am listening I nod my head as if I understand, but actually I have no clue what they are talking about.

I try to listen more carefully. I try to translate some of the words I am hearing, but then I get even more lost because I am a sentence behind them. I want to tell them, "I don't understand what you are talking about," but I don't want to be impolite and interrupt them. My only strategy is to nod my head, a gesture that communicates, "I understand."

Then they ask me a question that I only partly understand. I say something that I hope is an answer. When they look at me with big question marks on their faces, I realize that my guess was wrong. By this time, my wife has come to my rescue and answered for me.

Several years later, a language teacher told me that I could "train" native speakers to communicate with me. I could teach them how to change their speech so that I could understand them. I could learn to be patient with them until they adjusted to my way of speaking. But I didn't know that yet.

Several years after our dinner with the Müllers, I was visiting the family of one of my wife's sisters. Johanna, her husband Peter, and their two teenage sons Jakob and Sebastian live in village in a region of Bavaria called Oberpfalz, near where my wife grew up. It was a Sunday afternoon. I was sitting at the kitchen table with the family and a couple of their friends. We were eating cake and drinking coffee.

They were all speaking Oberpfälzisch. To my ear, Oberpfälzisch sounds like a completely different language but is really a dialect of German. It certainly is not the German I learned in my classes. So I was barely able to follow the general themes of the conversation, and it was impossible for me to get any details. My wife wasn't there to translate for me, but I felt a part of the conversation and a part of the family. Johanna and Peter have always welcomed me into their home.

I think—but I'm not sure—that the conversation was about neighbors and village life, a little gossip, a little news, laughing and reminiscing. One of

Johanna's friends suddenly used an expression, *ganz da kumma*. It stopped the conversation. No one at the table had ever heard this expression, and they asked her what it meant. She was amazed that they had never heard it. She swore that it is a common expression in Oberpfälzisch. The others swore that it must come from a different dialect. In mock outrage, they said, "That isn't Oberpfälzisch. It can't be." She was equally adamant. Everyone was laughing.

I wanted to know what they were talking about. So I turned to my nephew Jakob for help. He jumped up, grabbed a piece of paper, wrote *ganz da kumma* and then tried to tell me what it meant. I still didn't understand, and it didn't matter.

It didn't matter to me because I was enjoying the conversation, and it was a relief to realize that I was not the only one who didn't understand.

* * * * *

In my experience, Germany is a little like my father: a society that values cognitive skills more than affective and social skills, where objectivity is considered more important than subjectivity, where expertise is based on academic credentials and certification more than lived experience. Intelligence here seems to mean a particular kind of ability to use logic and data, and to think abstractly. Other kinds of intelligence, or what some people call "ways of knowing"—for example, through emotions, spirituality, and personal experience—don't seem to be valued here, at least not in ways that I recognize.

It seems to me, too, that some aspects of language ability aren't particularly valued here. In German schools, reading, writing and grammar are emphasized more than speaking. In my observation, many Germans are insecure using English for conversation, even if they received high marks in English classes. I think that they learned English as an academic subject rather than a practical tool for verbal communication. Maybe because of the emphasis on perfection, they are afraid that they will make mistakes.

In contrast, my friend Matho, who grew up in northeast India, speaks eight languages, including German. He feels comfortable using all these languages and doesn't worry about making mistakes. He is very socially competent. In India, his ability to communicate verbally is highly valued. But in Germany, Matho's multilingual skills are not particularly valued because he makes grammatical mistakes and doesn't write very well. Ironically, there is some talk now in Germany about the importance of social competence as a necessary job skill, but I doubt that this will translate into Matho being seen as an expert in communication.

The reality is that people like me, immigrants who speak very imperfect German, will probably be considered less qualified in comparison to Germans with formal education who speak perfectly, even though we actually may be more qualified. I believe that we are even considered less intelligent in comparison to highly educated native speaking Germans who have learned not only to speak formal German, but also the style of German used at the university (*Akademikerdeutsch*) and in official government correspondence (*Beamtendeutsch*).

In contrast, we immigrants speak with an accent, our vocabulary is limited, we make grammatical mistakes, we might use a mixture of slang, dialect, and formal German and sometimes throw in words from our native language. Few of us have had the opportunity to learn *Akademikerdeutsch* or *Beamtendeutsch*, so we are mystified by this kind of German.

When we listen to German, we probably need more time to process what is being said to us. So we listen carefully to a conversation, don't respond right away because we are catching up, then we need a little time to figure out how to respond in a conversation, and by that time the conversation has moved on. It's difficult for us to claim our place in the conversation, and if we say something, it might be difficult for a native speaker to understand us, and our words might sound a little odd to a native speaker. From the perspective of a native speaker, it could appear that our brains are, well, a little empty.

I suspect that few native German speakers will admit that they question our intelligence or consider us to be inferior, but I know it happens to immigrants in other places in the world. I've seen native English speakers in the U.S. ignore people who use English as a second language, and sometimes I've heard comments about the (in)abilities of non-native speakers. In fact, I have personally experienced being ignored in Germany, and later heard someone tell me that they were surprised to learn that I had something meaningful to say. So, I know that this phenomenon exists: immigrants using a second language, who don't speak like natives, are sometimes considered less competent, or simply inferior.

Based on the way that he responded to immigrants in the U.S., I suspect that my father believed that immigrants were less intelligent, and based on what he directly told me, I know that he believed that there was a connection between a person's character and their use of the English language. A "good" person speaks

English well. She or he speaks articulately, with perfect grammar, and, in the case of men, with a deep voice.

As a former military officer, my father believed a deep voice was essential for commanding respect. He had disparaging words for men who had a high pitch in their voice. I can still hear his imitation of men who he called "fairies." To make sure that I wouldn't become a fairy, my father taught how to make my voice deep.

Of course, there were several prejudices in his beliefs. One of these was that his version of English was "correct." He didn't realize, or want to accept, that what is considered "correct" English changes over time. Another prejudice was that "correct", or what other people call "standard" English, is somehow better than "non-standard" English, what people use every-day for conversation with friends and family.

My father's rule about using correct English and cultural rules here about using correct German reinforced each other. This combination was toxic for me.

Years later, when I was talking to a class at the University of Maryland about my experience learning German, Madeline Ehrman gave me another tip. Not only could I negotiate with teachers what I wanted to learn, she told me, "You need to get rid of your father's introjections about language."

So I decided to replace my father's critical voice with an encouraging voice. In this version, he told me, "I'm proud of how well you speak German. You take after your old man. You're pretty smart."

I think that's close to what he would have said if he hadn't been so obsessed with correcting my English. In fact, I think that he would have been envious that I am learning German. Learning other languages is something that he aspired to. He was excited when I gave him an audiocassette course in French, and then I watched him try to use French as a tourist in Paris when he was about 75 years old. About two years before he died at the age of 87, he bought a German dictionary and tried to write me a letter in German.

* * * * *

During the first few years of learning German, I was very aware of my father's voice and his rules. I wasn't aware of my mother's voice and her rules.

When I was a boy my mother taught ballroom dancing. Her mother, Viola Austin, taught ballroom, and ballet, for decades. Eventually my mother taught the classes by herself, but when I was a boy, they taught the classes together. So on Friday afternoons, when I was 12 years old, I was required to dress up and learn how to dance with a group of 50 other kids.

Of course, I had to be on my best behavior even when my friends acted out, like using rubber bands to shoot pieces of food across the room. My mother and grandmother tried hard to treat me like any other student, but they noticed whom I danced with and made comments about that when we got home. It was embarrassing.

The classes were much more than instruction in how to waltz and do the fox trot. From my mother and grandmother I learned about rhythm and big band music of the 1940's and 50's. I also learned about manners.

My mother continued her instruction in manners at home. I think she was a bit obsessive. She wanted an upper-class lifestyle, which we didn't have. My father worked behind the counter in a paint store, and her job teaching ballroom dancing was part-time. She didn't make much money, but she was determined to teach me to be polite according to what she thought were upper-class standards.

Andrea, one of my wife's friends, asked me to give her English lessons so that she could feel more confident speaking English. I met Andrea during one of my first visits to Germany, before I got married, and I had always liked her and wanted to get to know her better. I sensed that we could become good friends.

So I told her that I would help her with English if she would help me with German. She agreed. For over a year, beginning in 2007, we met weekly for three hours, first using one language and then the other. We were perfect partners for language learning. We simply talked about our lives and supported each other in finding ways to say what we wanted to say.

One day we talked about self-confidence and vulnerability, in German. It was exactly the kind of conversation that I had had with friends in the U.S. I missed doing this in my new language with German friends, and finally, I was able to do it.

At the end of the conversation, I said, "Thank you, Andrea, for this conversation."

"Why are you thanking me?"

"Because I'm glad that we had this conversation."

"You know, you do that a lot. Thanking me for things. It sounds strange to me. We don't do that in Germany."

"I know. But I think it's important to say thank you."

"Why?"

"I don't know. It just seems important to me. I think it's a way to appreciate another person. It's a gift, to be able to share our thoughts like this."

There was a pause in our conversation.

Andrea continued. "I'm glad you do that. My parents don't do that. One day my father was looking at one of my photographs and told me how I could improve it. I didn't like that he did that."

"What do you wish that he had done?"

"Tell me that it's a beautiful photograph."

"Of course!"

"Cooper, don't stop saying 'thank you' and giving compliments just because we don't do it. Please keep doing it. It makes me feel good."

There was another pause, and this time I spoke.

"I learned this from my mother. I wasn't very close to her, until a few years before she died. There was a lot distance between us. I thought she was too cold and formal. But I learned how to be polite."

For most of my life, I rebelled against my mothers rules for what she thought was the right way to live. It wasn't the way I wanted to live, and it caused conflict between us.

Nonetheless, in this moment with Andrea, I realized that what I had learned from my mom was helping me find my own identity in German. My mom's way of being polite was, for me, warmer and friendlier than what I was experiencing with Germans. Her lessons were giving me a way to make contact with strangers that sometimes—not always, but often enough—opened up doors to a different kind of relationship. I felt the coldness here, but my mom gave me a tool to make life a bit warmer.

As I write this, on a Friday afternoon, five years after her death, I wish that I could call her in the U.S. and thank her. Not only were her classes on Friday afternoon, but we had a routine in the last years of her life that I called her every Friday afternoon to chat. We both looked forward to those calls. She would have loved hearing that her son finally appreciated her lessons in manners.

Cooper Thompson

PART 2

FINDING MY VOICE:

successes and challenges on the path to fluency

First Steps

A few months after we moved into our new apartment, I went downstairs to check the mail and saw one of our neighbors coming home. I had not actually met him although I had seen him coming and going on the stairs in our apartment building. I decided that this was the time to introduce myself. I walked a few steps toward him and proudly started a conversation in German.

"Hi, I live upstairs. I'm Cooper Thompson."

He responded, "I am Krank."

I didn't know this at the time, but it is not typical in this region of Germany for people to be so forthright in introducing themselves. In fact, neighbors can go for years without ever really having a conversation with each other. If people do introduce themselves, they often use their last name only.

So, my neighbor had just told me his last name is Krank. But because I was expecting to hear two names, I was confused by what he said. I paused and translated Krank into English.

My conclusion: he just told me, "I am sick."

I did what anyone would do in my situation. I responded, "Tut mir leid dass Sie krank sind."

I just told him, "I am so sorry to hear that you are sick."

He gave me a strange look, then smiled, then said goodbye. I was not sure what had just happened, so I shrugged my shoulders and thought, "These Germans are a little odd and not very friendly."

Despite our first awkward conversation, we developed an easiness and friendliness with one another. He often spoke dialect, and I had a hard time following him, but we managed. Over the next couple of years, my wife and I became friends with Krank and his wife.

One night over dinner, they teased me about my first conversation with him. He had told his wife that he thought I was a little odd and overly friendly. I felt a little embarrassed as they reminded me how awkward I was at our first meeting, but I laughed with them.

I am sure that I made mistakes like this all the time. I was simply trying to make contact with people. Eva Hoffman described something similar in *Lost in Translation*.

> Because I'm not heard, I feel I'm not seen. My words often seem to baffle others. They are inappropriate, or forced, or just plain incomprehensible. People look at me with puzzlement; they mumble something in response – something that doesn't hit home. (p. 147)

In 1995, before I met my wife, I traveled to Ghana where I saw people who were highly skilled at making personal contact with strangers. Most Ghanaians are multi-lingual and can communicate across their ethnic and language differences. This is important, because there are many local languages spoken in Ghana in addition to the official language, English.

It is primarily an oral culture. I was told by Ghanaians that literacy is defined as the ability to read and write English, and almost half of the population is not literate according to that standard, and therefore deficient according to Western criteria. Of course, there isn't much need to read or write in the local languages, which for the most part have never been written down anyway.

So, it made me wonder: what if literacy were defined as the ability to communicate verbally with different kinds of people across language differences, and what if that was considered as valuable, if not more valuable, than the ability to read and write a language? If that were the standard of literacy, then many of us in so-called developed countries, especially where English is the native language, would realize we have a major problem because we haven't mastered the ability to communicate orally in several languages.

In the spring of 2004, my wife and I walked for three weeks in Spain on a section of the Camino de Santiago de Compostela, an ancient pilgrimage route that crosses Europe. As we passed through villages, following the small markers with a blue scallop shell pointing the way, it was clear to the local people that we were pilgrims on our way to Santiago in northwest Spain. They greeted us and sometimes asked us to pray for them when we reached our destination.

Sometimes people wanted to have a conversation with us. We tried telling them that our Spanish was really bad, and we didn't understand what they were saying. It didn't seem to matter. They went right on talking to us. I wish that I had responded in English and told them about our trip and who we were. I wonder what would have happened. Instead of feeling awkward, we might have understood each other. At least, we might felt a bond between us.

The kind of conversation that happened in Ghana and on the Pilgrimage almost never happened in Nürnberg. Seldom did anyone approach me. If I initiated contact, people might give me a one-word response and most of the time didn't seem interested in having a conversation. My first attempt at a conversation with Krank turned out to be typical of what I experienced.

Like Eva Hoffman, I wanted to be seen and heard even if my German wasn't very good. However, it is a skill to know how to listen to someone who is using a second language, and I didn't find many native German speakers in Nürnberg who had this skill or who seemed to want contact with me. I didn't know how to engage with native German speakers in a way that they would listen to me and take me seriously. Sometimes I wasn't very patient with them and didn't give them time to adjust to me, but I was trying.

* * * * *

In the fall of 2005, I heard about a self-help group in Nürnberg for people dealing with addiction. When I had lived in Boston, I had attended a similar group on Wednesday nights for several years. I missed the group. Luckily, the Nürnberg group met in my neighborhood and, by coincidence, on Wednesday night. I thought it was a good omen and decided to join. I was excited.

I was also nervous. How was I going to do this in German? I didn't think that I had the ability to talk about really personal things.

I gathered the courage to go. I was welcomed. And it wasn't easy.

Sometimes we read together from a text. I took my turn in the circle, and I felt embarrassed about the way that I stumbled over words that were way beyond the vocabulary in my upper beginners' class. When I got my chance to share something about myself, I didn't have the vocabulary to describe my thoughts and feelings.

When others shared what was going on in their lives, I couldn't follow what they were saying. Sometimes they spoke fast, sometimes in dialect, sometimes in slang. I caught bits and pieces, but I was mostly lost. The first few times I went, I felt like crying. I thought, I don't belong in this group.

But I kept going, and after I had been there a few times, I felt a bit more comfortable. People were really glad to see me when I came in the room. One evening, I shared something that the others seemed to understand. They even laughed with me when I said something that I thought was funny.

After going to the group for about six months, a member of the group told me one night, "Cooper, you bring a wonderful *geist* (spirit) to this group."

I told her, "Thank you." I accepted it as a compliment.

I was, however, puzzled. Why would she say this? I didn't say much in the group. I didn't see how I contributed very much.

The next day I realized that maybe she was talking about a quality that I brought to the group that had nothing to do with how much I said or how much I understood. I do know that I pay close attention to people when they are talking. I try to empathize.

Maybe the spirit she saw had something to do with who I am, instead of what I am able to do. The next day I wrote in my journal, "Living in Germany is an opportunity for me to learn about "being" instead of "doing."

As I continued to attend the group, I got other compliments, some direct, some indirect. One person told me about the positive energy I brought to the group. Another told me that I was courageous. One night the theme that I suggested for our open discussion—powerlessness—was chosen by the group. On other nights, comments that I had made were repeated by other group members.

One night, there was a lively discussion. I kept hearing the word *demut*. I didn't know this word. I started to obsess about the meaning of *demut* and then told myself to relax and remember that I would eventually understand what they were talking about.

So I simply listened. After 15 minutes it came to me: *demut* means humility. I chuckled to myself: not knowing is a form of humility. Then I took my turn speaking.

I told the group what I had been experiencing for the last 15 minutes.

"*Demut*. This is a new word for me. I think tonight is the first time I've heard this word. When you were talking about *demut*, at first I didn't understand. But then I realized what *demut* means."

"*Demut* is not something I learned from my father. When I was boy, he told me that I always had to have an answer. It was not okay to say 'I don't know.'

However, living in Germany, there are so many things that I don't know. I have many opportunities to practice *demut*."

Sometimes when I was speaking German and trying to find the words I wanted to say, I would avoid looking at someone's face. It distracted me. I had to look away. However, as I talked about humility, I felt confident enough to look at the group. I saw some people nodding, and the person who spoke after me referred to what I had said.

As I walked home from the group, I thought about my father's rule and how it had served me well in terms of self-confidence and creativity. I had learned that I could always come up with an answer, but it also led to me being arrogant, thinking that I knew all the answers. I thought I was an expert at times when I didn't really know what I was talking about.

On another night, the topic was perfection. Some of us in the group had tried to be perfect in our lives, and of course we had made many mistakes and sometimes hurt other people in the process. Acknowledging our mistakes was difficult for us, but essential. We were realizing that we would continue to make mistakes.

"You know," I told the group, "I make a lot of mistakes when I speak German. Sometimes I want to speak faster, and sometimes I am afraid that you won't be patient if I speak slowly. But if I speak too fast, I lose myself. I don't want that. I have done that too much in my life. I want to go at my own speed."

A few minutes later, after someone else had spoken, I took another turn. "Maybe it's good that I live here now, and that there are so many things that I don't know. Maybe it's good to have to listen and to wait. Maybe it's good for me to slow down. Maybe I will understand some things in a new way."

* * * * *

My wife was looking for a new dentist, and I didn't have a dentist here, so we went together to a man whose office was near our apartment. I didn't feel confident going to a doctor by myself, so I was happy to go with her. She sat in the examining room with me, ready to translate when I needed it.

I knew that I should use *Sie* with the dentist, but I felt more comfortable using *du*. So, I used *du* with him. In the U.S., I was on a first name basis with my dentist. If someone is probing around in my mouth, I'd rather feel a little less like strangers. Other people might want some social distance, but not me.

I was nervous using German with the dentist, but it turned out fine. I felt reasonably comfortable with him, my teeth got cleaned, and I didn't have any cavities. My wife didn't need to translate.

As we were walking home, she said to me, "You were great with him, and I'm amazed how friendly he was with you."

"Well, I was friendly with him."

"Maybe it's because you're a man. He was reserved with me."

"Could be. But you could have been friendlier with him. You were so formal. I heard you using *Sie* with him. You could have used *du*."

I may as well have suggested that she ask the guy to take out all her teeth.

"You can't do that here! You have to be formal with doctors."

"No, you don't. I wasn't formal with him. I was using *du*."

"You don't understand. I can't do that."

I was amazed to hear this. Of course, I knew that the distinction between *Sie* and *du* was important, but I hadn't realized that Germans were so deeply conditioned in their use of *Sie* and *du*. Or, at least, my wife was. I had been discounting the fact that I am an older man from the U.S., an outsider, who could get away with being informal and with breaking cultural rules.

Although the dentist was a nice guy, I wanted to keep using my dentist in Boston. I had known him for years, and we had developed a friendship. So, whenever I flew back to the U.S., I scheduled an appointment with him.

But several years later, in 2008, after I stopped traveling to the U.S., I needed to find a dentist here. This time, I made the appointment by myself. I found a woman who had been trained at Tufts University in Boston and had worked in the U.S. for several years. I hadn't planned on speaking English with her, but she wanted to, so we did.

It made a big difference in the content of our conversation. Unlike any German doctor I had met, she told me a lot about herself. Maybe she just wanted to practice her English, but I really think using English made the conversation more informal. Without being aware of it, I suspect that we were using cultural norms from the U.S. that allowed us to reduce the social distance that was typical for German culture.

Since I didn't have to worry about the decision to use *du* or *Sie*, I decided to take a risk in another way.

"I was friends with my dentist in Boston," I told her.

"Yeah, things are so much more informal there."

"They are. I called him by his first name."

"That happened with me, too, when I worked in the clinic. Some of my patients called me Anita."

I paused, and then asked her, "Could I use your first name?"

She paused, but not for long. "You're the first client in 15 years who has asked me that. Sure."

I thanked her. "That makes it more comfortable for me."

"But I need to ask you a favor. When you call here, please don't tell my receptionist that you'd like to make an appointment to see Anita. She will not like that. She is typically German and very formal. If she knows that you are informal with me, I will hear about it from her."

As I was leaving the office, Anita accompanied me to the door. We passed by the receptionist. I shook Anita's hand and said, "Vielen dank, Frau Doktor Stein."

* * * * *

When I listen to native German speakers, if I don't understand exactly what they are saying, I listen for the themes and context, and then I fill in my understanding of what is being said. I make assumptions all the time about words and phrases that I don't understand. I had to do that constantly when I was a beginner, and I still do it, even after years of learning German. It is very rare that I understand every word in a conversation.

There are actually not many new things I hear. Most of what people say I have already experienced in some form, or heard about, or read about. I think this is a big advantage I have as an older language learner.

Of course, this is not always true; there are times when I think that I understand, and then I find out that my assumptions are wrong. On the other hand, I am struck with how often my assumptions are correct, or correct enough, so that I can follow the conversation without needing to interrupt for clarification of what I don't understand. When I can, I choose situations where I will have a better chance of understanding what people are saying. If I go to a lecture, for example, I pick those that are interesting to me and where I already have some experience with the topic.

On a Friday evening in 2006, I decided to go to a talk, "Recovering from Trauma through Spirituality," given by a psychotherapist I knew. My wife and I had met with Ulrike a few times in our first year of marriage. I had always liked her. So, I was excited to go to her talk, but I was also scared, as I often was, of going to an event where I probably wouldn't know anyone. My wife had to work, so I went by myself.

When I arrived, Ulrike was happy to see me and excited that so many people had come to her talk. She was also nervous but for a different reason.

"There are many therapists here tonight, colleagues of mine, and some of them will be skeptical about what I have to say. I don't like giving talks, but I think it's important for me to share with them some of my thoughts."

"I know. I have the same feeling. I don't like giving talks, but sometimes I have to."

Then she said gently, "I hope that you can understand my talk."

"Oh, I'll understand what I can, and I'm sure that I will enjoy what you say."

I sat in the front row. From experience I know that I have a better chance of understanding a speaker if I am physically closer.

I found the talk fascinating. I listened carefully to Ulrike, responded with nods and even made a comment at one point. She gave me lots of eye contact. I understood some of her talk, or at least I think I understood. The concepts were not unfamiliar to me, and so I figured out some of the words that I didn't recognize. I wrote down about a dozen words that I didn't understand, so that I could find out what they meant when I got home. This had become a habit: I carried a little notebook with me for German vocabulary.

At the end of the talk, I went up to her, thanked her very much. She also thanked me for having come.

The next week, Ulrike had an appointment with my wife. When she came home, my wife told me, "Ulrike said that your presence at her talk felt really supportive to her. The way you listened to her gave her strength to say what she wanted to say."

"She told you that?"

"Yes, that's exactly what she said."

"But how can that be? Ulrike knows my level of German, and she knows that her talk was a stretch for me. I didn't really say anything."

Then I remembered something that I had experienced before: that the way I listen could be more important than understanding completely what someone is telling me. Maybe I can listen without being so dependent on words. I'm sure I did this as a baby, before I understood the words that people were using, and I have had this experience as an adult.

About 15 years ago, in Colorado, I was leading a workshop on oppression. An older Mexican American woman wanted to share something with a younger Mexican American woman. It had to do with the importance of remembering who you are in your own language and culture, in the face of pressure to assimilate. The older woman had worked for years in a major U.S. corporation, was successful, and had proudly held on to her cultural identity and often spoke Spanish at work. The younger woman was also working in a corporation, but getting pressure to assimilate to corporate culture. She was feeling lost, unsure how to go forward with her career, and trying to figure out what was important to her.

As the older woman began speaking with the younger woman, I suddenly thought to myself, they should have this conversation in Spanish. So I turned to her and asked, "Would you like to speak Spanish instead of English?"

She smiled. "Yes. That would be wonderful."

The group watched and listened in silence while the two women had a long, intense conversation. Toward the end, the younger woman cried, and the older woman held her.

A white man, Robert, who had recently moved to the U.S. from South Africa was sitting next to the two women. While they talked, he sat quietly, leaning forward in his chair, listening carefully, occasionally nodding. I thought, this is amazing. He knows Spanish. I'm surprised that a white South African speaks Spanish.

Later, I asked Robert where he had learned Spanish.

"I don't speak Spanish."

"You don't?"

"No."

"But you looked like you understood."

"I was just listening carefully."

In fact, none of the other participants in the workshop spoke Spanish, certainly not enough to follow the conversation between the two women. Nonetheless, the group's ability to listen and be patient created an environment where the two women felt supported.

Sometimes when I am listening to people and not understanding their words, I remember what Robert did. In those moments, I have a sense that he is with me, showing me a way to be patient, and a way to simply stay present.

In 2007, I was asked to work with a group of people in Frankfurt who were getting certified as trainers. I would be teaching them in English how to facilitate workshops similar to the ones I had led in the U.S. I was pleased to be asked.

I had been reluctant, however, to say "Yes." The organizers of the program told me that some of the participants' English ability was not very high. I didn't know if I would be able to work effectively with people in this kind of situation.

I accepted the work and encouraged people right from the start to use their native language whenever they wanted or needed to. Not only did I hear German spoken during the workshop, but also Turkish, Russian, and Hindi from time to time. Sometimes there were conversations in three languages simultaneously: Gül said something in Turkish, Sabine responded in English, and Jutta added something in German. I spoke English most of the time but used German when I felt confident enough.

After the workshop, I received feedback that the participants felt I had really listened to them and understood them. At the same time, they knew that my German was not that good, and my Turkish, Russian, and Hindi were non-existent.

That same year, I was asked to help lead a week-end seminar for a group of German men. My co-leader was another man from the U.S. The seminar was advertised as being in English, but shortly after we began, two men objected to our using English, due to their lack of fluency.

I suggested to my co-leader that we try to use German even though I was nervous about that. His German was better than mine, but he was more nervous than I was. We did what we could in German and asked members of the group to help us translate when we needed to use English.

I was surprised at how much I could communicate in German and how creative I was in teaching some difficult concepts. I tried to find examples, tell stories, use gestures and pantomime, engage the group in helping me find the words to describe things—I did whatever I could to communicate. It worked, or at least it worked enough, so that the participants understood what we were saying. In their evaluations, most of them told us that the seminar had been successful.

When I first suggested that we use German in this seminar, I didn't know how I would do it. I simply believed that it was important to use German, and I was willing to take the risk.

That was a strategy I would use again and again. I dove into situations without knowing if I would be able to communicate.

Confidence

About three years after I started taking German classes, I made an important decision. I stopped saying, "My German is terrible."

I had regularly started conversations with "My German is terrible" as a way to indirectly say to whoever I was speaking with, "Please be patient with me." With time, I found there were a few problems with my conversation starter. It didn't necessarily get me the patience I wanted; my German wasn't really that bad, so the statement wasn't accurate; and most important, it was probably keeping me stuck in a mindset that I couldn't learn this language.

Instead, I decided to tell myself that my German is good enough. That was true. It was far from perfect, I still had much to learn, and it was good enough for my daily life. It became a mantra: my German is good enough. My German is good enough. My German is good enough. Praising myself felt better than criticizing myself.

My wife and I went for a hike one day with two other couples, people she had known for a long time. One of the men, Bernard, didn't seem like he wanted to listen to me; as I talked with him, he seemed distracted, looking away instead of at me. It reminded me of being at a party, where my conversation partner is looking for someone more important or interesting to talk with.

Previously, I would have thought, Bernard is not interested in talking with me because my German isn't good enough. This time, though, I thought, it's his problem, not mine. Nothing is wrong with me. He just doesn't know how to listen. I think I have some interesting things to say, so if he doesn't want to listen to me, it's his loss.

I made a point of walking next to him for a while, asking him questions and listening, and I took the chance of sharing some of my thoughts with him even as I was aware that he might not be interested. I wanted to talk, too. I think my German was pretty good that day.

Sometimes I had the sense that my language ability had taken a leap forward. In the spring of 2006, we had different friends come to our apartment three nights in a row. It used to be that I would be tired after one or two hours. I would run into the kitchen on the pretense of cooking or washing dishes when actually I needed to get a break from using German. On these three nights, however, I hung out with people for several hours and didn't need to run off. I enjoyed being with them.

A month later, I had a conversation on the phone with Karin and Jonas. Karin went to school with my wife; I first met Karin in 2000 on my second trip to Germany. She wanted to check me out, to make sure that my wife wasn't involved with some weird guy who was unknown to her friends. I passed the test, and three years later she and her husband Jonas came to our wedding.

When I first met Karin, I hadn't even considered learning German, and fortunately she spoke English. But as I spent more time with her and Jonas, and as I began to learn German, we used a mix of both languages. Then, on June 28, 2006, I wrote in my journal, "Today I talked for 20 minutes on the phone with Karin and Jonas. We only spoke German. They complimented me big time. During the call, I never felt embarrassed about making mistakes or not understanding something they said. I just talked and talked. They were amazed, and so am I."

The next week my wife and I went to their house for dinner. I had brought an Indian dish that Karin has a particular fondness for: chicken in red pepper sauce. As she and I stood in the kitchen, making the final preparations for dinner, I spoke English with her. Even though she was now a friend and it felt easy to be with her, I was tired and wanted to use English. I didn't feel ready to speak German. I needed to warm up.

As we sat down to dinner, we all begin to use German, and for the rest of the evening, we spoke only German. It wasn't a decision we made; it just happened. At one point we were all laughing at me; I was talking about the dish I had brought, and I mispronounced the word for *chicken*. It came out as *little dogs*: we were eating puppies in red pepper sauce.

I made many other mistakes that evening: words I mispronounced, words in the wrong place in a sentence, wrong endings for adjectives, and wrong verb tenses. Sometimes I heard my mistakes and chose to continue rather than become obsessed with them. Sometimes I asked for a correction. Sometimes I repeated what I had said, cleaned up the mistake, and then continued.

Although my father might have thought that it was possible to speak perfectly, I was beginning to realize that I would always make mistakes in German. If I tried to be perfect, I would put pressure on myself. I wanted to feel comfortable, and be playful with German. I was slowly changing my father's rule, and creating my own: my goal is communication, not perfection.

At the end of dinner, Karin and Jonas again complimented me. "Your German is getting better all the time. We're impressed!" On this evening, I was successful in reaching my goal. I had fun.

Later that year, my wife's brother Klaus and his wife Rosie had twins. They asked us to be godparents. A few months later I attended the baptism in the church in my wife's village. The church is next to the house where she grew up and where her parents still live. As a child, my wife woke up each day to the bells ringing in the church steeple.

After the baptism, we went to the next village for a big family dinner at a guest house. I was sitting at one end of a long table. Most of the boys and men were, for some reason, clustered at my end of the table. Two nephews, Sebastian and Jakob—Johanna and Peter's sons—were to my right. Klaus was to my left. Further down the table were my wife, Rosie, and the rest of the extended family.

Klaus and I had the twins, Mattius and Katharina, in our laps. I held one of them, Klaus held the other, we switched from time to time. When they started to cry, we gave them a bottle or a pacifier or rocked them. Periodically we had to give some attention to the twin's four year old sister Lisa who was happy to have a brother and sister but who wasn't going to be ignored.

It was perfect for me. I was talking with my nieces and nephews. They didn't care if I made mistakes or even if I made sense. I love holding babies, and Rosie and Klaus trust me with their kids. Katharina and Mattius listened to me, intensely, their three-month-old brains trying to make sense of what I was saying. Lisa, Jakob, and Sebastian had lots to tell me, and I listened to them, intensely, as if I understood, even though most of the time I didn't. Of course, they were all speaking Oberpfälzisch.

My conversations with the kids were punctuated by laughter from Klaus. He is a farmer and mechanic. I really like him. He often laughs, and today he was happy to be with his family, happy to have three kids. Like his four year old daughter, he talked to me as if I understood perfectly what he was saying.

Previously, at these family gatherings, I had felt uncomfortable. With the exception of my brother-in-law Peter, no one could speak English. When they were together as a family, they all spoke dialect, and I was trying to speak standard German. But that day I was enjoying myself. My language ability had never been an issue. They simply accepted me as part of the family. For them, being together and enjoying each other's company was important. Impressing other people with words was not.

* * * * *

In late summer of 2007, I registered for another intensive German class: Mittlestufe 2 (Intermediate level 2). On the last day of class, we took a written exam. When we were done, we each privately checked our answers against the correct ones. I got over 70% correct, and so I passed.

Then Astrid, our teacher, made a startling announcement. "You are now fluent." Collectively we responded, "Huh?" No one believed it. We had puzzled looks on our faces. What could she possibly mean? We knew we still had so much to learn. We felt awkward using German. It was still hard work to use this language. But Astrid insisted that we were fluent.

I felt a slight sense of pride, but mostly I felt self-doubt. I didn't believe I was fluent. Although I had never thought about what fluency actually means, I assumed it meant something like having a big, rich vocabulary that comes effortlessly out of my mouth. If I were fluent, I would be able to express all of my thoughts and feelings. I would feel completely comfortable and confident.

But now, looking back, I think what Astrid meant was that we had passed a test based on a European standard of second language proficiency. This standard is a work in progress and an attempt to describe a person's competence in the use of a second language. It assumes that someone learning a second language is in a process of learning, not that they have arrived at the end of a journey and can speak perfectly. So according to experts somewhere in Europe, our passing this test meant that our language proficiency was good enough to describe us as fluent.

This description of fluency didn't match my own internal standard of fluency, a standard based on my skills in English, the language that I had grown up and used for almost 60 years. No wonder I didn't think I was fluent.

That fall, I made several trips to the U.S. for work. I hadn't been there for about nine months, so there was lots of catching up to do with friends.

"How's your German?" they asked me. "You must be fluent by now."

"My last teacher told me I was, but I don't think I am. I'm much more aware of what I can't say than what I can say. Yet, if I look at day-to-day life, I do okay."

Back in Germany, I got together one night for dinner with some other native English speakers living in Nürnberg. A young woman from the U.S. who had only been in Germany a year, asked me about my German, and after I gave her a description of my ability, she said, "You're fluent." I heard her, but I still didn't believe it.

So, I went back to some of the research I had found on learning a second language, and I read that the experts have different views about fluency. Some experts measure second language ability against the standard of native speakers, with the goal of sounding like a native speaker. That was the standard I had apparently adopted for myself.

Other experts write about acquisition and competence in a second language: the ability to communicate based on the situation that you're in. This means that you might make lots of grammatical mistakes, have a small vocabulary, and speak with a foreign accent, but you can more or less successfully communicate what you want and need to. This seems closer to the European standards.

Then I read something that challenged my standard of fluency even more: many people who use a second language create their own way to use the language. I had heard immigrants doing this in the U.S. I knew that people around the world did this when they were forced to use a language imposed by colonizers. One day I heard a Chinese woman doing this at the neighborhood grocery store she owns with her husband. Talking with her son on the phone, she used both Chinese and German in the same sentence, and seemed to create her own language from a mixture of the two languages.

I shopped there frequently and had become friendly with her. So, I asked her about this. She laughed and said, "Oh yeah, we do that all the time." If I had listened really carefully to her and had understood Chinese, I suspect that I would have heard a mixture of grammar and syntax from both Chinese and German as if she and her son were blending the two languages together.

After a few more years here, I began to do that with my wife, too. One day she asked me in English if I were hungry, and I answered spontaneously in English, "I have no hunger." Without thinking about it, I had used German grammar to express something in English. Or we would make up new words in the other person's language, based on what we thought they should sound like. So, it became common to use both German and English in the same sentence.

One day my wife told me that Johanna and Peter's family, where I had learned the expression *ganz da kumma*, had started using a expression that they say they had learned from me: *Alles ist in Schlamassel*. It means "everything's a mess," or you could translate it as "everything's fucked up." Out of curiosity, I looked up *Schlamassel* in an online dictionary. It can also mean "dog's breakfast."

I don't know where I first heard this expression. I am pretty sure it was here in Germany, but *Schlamassel* sounded like some of the Yiddish words I heard from Jewish friends in Boston. It had a familiar sound to it. So, I started saying, *Alles ist in Schlamassel*, even when it probably didn't fit the context, simply because I liked saying it. It felt good in my mouth. Another *Ich habe Schwein gehabt* moment.

I must have used it around my in-laws. They thought it sounded cool—or maybe really strange. Maybe they heard it as, "Everything is like a dog's breakfast," and that was so ridiculous that it was worth repeating.

I really don't care what it means or what they hear. What I think is really cool is that I've already had an impact on the German language—at least, in one home in a village in Oberpfalz in Bavaria.

* * * * *

A few months after I was declared fluent, I was skimming through the catalogue of courses offered through the local Volkshochschule (Adult Education Center) and saw something that caught my attention: Theatre Games for Beginners. I had always been curious about theatre games, but really knew nothing about them. I suspected it would be a challenge for me to do this course in German, and like I often do, I took the risk and registered for a weekend workshop.

On a Friday night, 15 of us gathered in a large room with a stage. We ranged in age from 17 to 58. As usual, I was the oldest, and in this group, the only person who was not a native German speakers. After a brief round where we each introduced ourselves, Stefan, our teacher, told us the most important ground rule for the weekend. "You have the right to say 'no' and the obligation to say 'no' to any activity we do. Don't participate in an activity if you don't feel comfortable doing it."

I was pretty nervous as we started our introductions, but when Stefan told us that we could say "no", I immediately relaxed. I had never had a teacher give such clear reassurance in the face of the fear I often felt. I could choose when to participate and when not to.

During the weekend, I participated in all of the activities, even when they were way over my head. I never hesitated to jump in and do what Stefan suggested.

The activities got more challenging as the weekend came to a close. On Sunday afternoon, we paired up. Uli and I were partners. Stefan told us to interview each other for five minutes. Then, each pair would take a turn on the stage, in a talk show format, and the other participants would be the audience.

However, there was a catch: I would have to act like I were Uli, and she would have to act like she were me. Moreover, the audience would be asking the questions. We would need to convince them that I was Uli, and that she was Cooper.

So, when Marcus or Karina in the audience asked, "Cooper, what is your favorite food?" Uli had to answer, and I couldn't react even though the question had been directed to "Cooper." Or, when Oliver or Sabine asked Uli, "What do like to do on weekends?" I had to respond spontaneously and naturally as if I were used to being called "Uli." When we had interviewed each other, Uli and I hadn't talked about our favorite foods or what we did on the weekend, so we both had to make things up, and quickly, and sound convincing.

I don't think I gave very good answers, and I reacted a couple of times to questions asked to Cooper. Nonetheless, as we did a final closure and feedback round, I felt proud. I had attended a weekend course in German on a topic I know nothing about. I had fun even though it was a huge challenge. The movement, the playfulness, the combination of fantasy and reality, and the support from other participants—all of that made for a great weekend.

It was the best German class I had ever taken.

* * * * *

In the U.S., I owned a small cabin in Vermont. It was a place for me to escape to. I loved being in the woods. I missed the cabin. My wife and I both love hiking. So, we started looking for something similar in a hilly area north of Nürnberg called Fränkische Schweiz.

In 2008, after a year of searching, we bought a small house in a village called Höfles. It needed lots of work. In fact, one of my wife's brothers, who does renovations, told us that the place was worthless. Still, it had southern exposure and a view, and we were able to buy it for half of what the owner wanted. Over the next two years, we spent twice as much on renovations.

I was excited to have a place in the country and scared about the renovations. I did a lot of this kind of work in the U.S. In my 20's I worked as a carpenter, and later I renovated a couple of houses, doing a lot of the work myself. But in Germany? The building materials are different, I didn't know any contractors who could help me, and I didn't have any tools here. We had never had a lesson in my German classes about home renovation, so I didn't have the vocabulary I needed.

After nine months of work, I felt a little bit more confident. With the help of some contractors, I had accomplished a lot. I still had plenty to learn, and I couldn't always remember some of the words for things. But the house looked great.

I had built relationships with three carpenters, a plumber, and the owner of a local saw mill. They seemed to accept me like one of the locals: they were happy to see me, we chatted about the weather, we drank beer together, and most importantly, I got teased like I was one of the guys. I even helped the carpenters when they suddenly needed an extra hand for a couple of days on a house they were building. I'm not sure how much help I was, but it felt great to think that I could do this work, in German.

Sometimes, when I told friends in the U.S. about the renovations I was doing, I automatically used German words like *Zimmerman*, *Dachfenster*, and *Estrich* to refer to the carpenter I was working with, the skylight we had installed, or the concrete I had poured. Then I had to pause in midsentence to search my brain for the English equivalent so that the person on the other end of the phone would understand what I was talking about.

My wife and I realized that we would need a car for doing the renovations and schlepping materials back and forth from Nürnberg to Höfles. It's only 35 kilometers, but we were naïve to think that we would be able to do this with our bicycles and the train. Up until this point, we had chosen to live without a car.

We heard about a 24-year-old car owned by an older woman. She was the original owner and in the previous ten years had driven it an average of 1000 kilometers per year. She was asking 1300 euros, but after a test drive, we offered 600 because I sensed something was wrong with the engine. It didn't have the power it should have. I had a hunch what it was, and I thought that 600 euros was a fair price given the repairs we would have to make. When I told her that something was wrong, she worried that she was selling a car with problems and wouldn't accept more than 500.

So, we bought a 1983 Nissan Prairie, perfect for hauling building materials to the house and taking used stuff to the recycling center. No one in Nürnberg had a car like ours.

I took Prairie, as we affectionately called her, to a small independent auto shop in the neighborhood. In addition to a new muffler, the mechanic figured it needed an exhaust manifold and a thermostat. A crack in the manifold and the fact that the engine wasn't warming up seemed to be causing the loss of power.

I know a little bit about cars. I used to work on them when I was younger, and so I understood what the mechanic told me even though I had never heard of some of the words he used. I didn't try to memorize them. How often would I need to use *Schalldämpfer*, *Abgaskrümmer*, and *Temperaturregler*?

Finding a thermostat was easy, but the muffler and exhaust manifold were another story. The parts manager made calls to distributors and junk yards but couldn't find anyone who had heard of a Nissan Prairie let alone had parts for it. The mechanic's solution was to try to weld the crack in the manifold and then find a muffler that was a close fit and weld that, too. It would be cheaper that way, and hopefully, it would work.

The mechanic told me he had an old friend (I'm not sure if I heard old friend or old man) who was an expert welder. Since it was not clear when he would have time to do this job, it would be best to return in a week and leave the car with them. I was in no hurry.

The next week I went to the shop and the parts manager greeted me by name. "Good morning, Herr Thompson."

I was amazed. "You remember my name?"

"Of course, I remember you. I had to make all those calls to find the parts for your car," he said, laughing.

He told me to fill in a form and then asked me, "Where is the registration for the car?

"It's in the car, in the ... " I stopped because I didn't know the word for glove compartment.

I started to giggle and told him, "Ich weiss nicht das Wort, aber es klingt wie Handschuhabteilung." (I don't know the word, but it sounds like glove department.)

He laughed. "I understand! The thing in front of the passenger seat."

"Yes! Exactly. What is the word for that?"

"*Handschuhfach.*"

I wasn't that far off.

* * * * *

In November, 2008, I traveled to Boston for the first time in almost a year. I had been exchanging emails with a language learning expert, Dr. Rebecca Oxford. She was teaching at the University of Maryland, and I had read on-line about some pioneering work that she had done on language learning strategies. She has identified hundreds of different ways that second language learners use on their own, consciously or unconsciously, to learn a language.

I was eager to meet Rebecca, so I offered to travel to Maryland. She asked me to give a presentation to her class on second language learning about my experience learning German. I was both nervous and excited. I was not an expert on second language learning although I was eager to talk about my own experience.

I arrived a few minutes early for the class. Rebecca was not there yet, but waiting outside the classroom was Dr. Yalun Zhou, a Chinese-American woman and former doctoral student of Rebecca's. We introduced ourselves. She knew that I would be giving a presentation and asked me casually about my experience learning German. When I described my ability to use German, she told me, "You're bilingual."

I said, "I am?"

It had been a year since Astrid told me I was fluent, and I hadn't fully accepted it. Now a stranger had told me that I was bilingual.

I gave my presentation. I told some stories. I talked about the difficulties I had experienced, and I emphasized the emotional and social aspects of learning German. It was well received.

Rebecca made some comments about the strategies I had been using to overcome my difficulties. One of her colleagues, Dr. Madeline Ehrman, described the kind of learning environment that would work best for me. The students asked lots of questions, and nodded in agreement as I described my experiences. They understood.

I told the class about the conversation I had had with Yalun and added, "Being bilingual has been a goal in my life for at least 30 years. I didn't expect to be bilingual in German and English – I wanted it to be Spanish and English – but things didn't turn out that way."

I was not quite ready to say that I was bilingual, but I was ready to "try on" my new identity. I felt proud. For the first time, I had the sense that there were people who understood what I had been experiencing and who might be able to support me in getting past the difficulties I had been having with learning German.

Soon I was on a Lufthansa flight back to Germany, watching a French film about a group of people walking on the Camino de Santiago de Compostela. I was listening to the film in French, not understanding everything, but because I had walked the path and because I knew some French, I was able to follow the story. The terrain was familiar.

The French I was hearing in my headphones must have been stimulating a part of my brain where French is stored because when a flight attendant came by to ask me which dinner choice I wanted, I responded automatically in French. Then I suddenly realized that she had asked me in German—we had spoken German up to this point in the flight. But now, with French in my head, I couldn't find the words in German to say what I wanted to say! I laughed and tried to explain my dilemma to her in a mix of French, German, and English. She laughed with me.

And then, an amazing thought occurred to me: maybe I'm trilingual. Or at least I could be with a little practice. If that's possible, I might be able to reach my life of goal of being fluent in Spanish, too.

Recognition

I went to the doctor's office one day. I had been there a few times, but on this day I went without an appointment because I only needed a prescription and could get that from the receptionist. When I walked into the office, she greeted me by name. I couldn't believe it: someone knew my name. It felt great.

I was beginning to get noticed. The woman at the cheese counter in a local grocery store smiled when I came in and asked me if I wanted cheddar cheese, like I usually did. The butcher at the Friday local grower's market greeted me and asked me how I was. The man who sold homemade ice cream at the same market called out, "Hallo, Herr Thompson," when he saw me coming. I had once telephoned him to asked him if he could bring some pistachio ice cream the following Friday to the market. It was my wife's favorite flavor.

In the Hauptmarkt (main square) in the center of Nürnberg, there is an open air food market every day. As I walked through the Hauptmarkt, I went out of my way to make personal contact with some of the people where I regularly shopped even if I didn't need to buy something from them on that day.

One day I stopped to say hello to Ruth, a young woman selling locally-grown vegetables. She was only there once a week, so I didn't see her very often. The last time I had seen her I needed her advice on which type of potato to buy when I was cooking a casserole for my sister-in-law Johanna's 40th birthday party.

Ruth has a big smile and lots of energy. She was excited to see me on that day and wanted to know how the potatoes worked out. I told her, and then asked her if we could use *du*. She responded, "We already decided that a while back." I didn't remember that, but I liked that she was so relaxed and decisive.

As I talked to her and looked at the produce she had, I got inspired to cook something for lunch. I told her what I was thinking: a couple of South Indian vegetarian dishes.

"That sounds tasty," she told me.

So I asked her, "How late will be you here at the market?"
"Until 1pm."
"I'll go home and cook, and then I'll bring you back a hot lunch."
"You will?"
"Sure, why not?" I was sure that no one had ever done what I was proposing.
"That would be great. Then I'll have something for my husband and me."

I went home, cooked, and a couple of hours later walked back to the Hauptmarkt with three containers for Ruth. It was a little like being in India and delivering tiffins at lunch time. As I walked, I felt happy. This was the kind of contact with people that I had been missing here.

This produce stand was my favorite place to shop in the Hauptmarkt. Most of the time Hilde, an older woman, was there. Hilde didn't seem as easy going as Ruth. She gave me the impression that she was more interested in selling produce than chatting with customers. She didn't want me touching the produce, whereas Ruth let me pick out I wanted.

Usually I went alone to shop, but one day my wife was with me. While I was on one side Hilde's stall, she leaned over the carrots and whispered to my wife, "Your husband is so sweet."

"Really? You think so?"

"Oh, yeah, he is really sweet. Where is he from, and how did you two meet?"

"He's from the U.S., and we met there."

"You are lucky. He is sweet. He is always so friendly when he shops here."

I hadn't heard any of this. We paid for our onions, carrots, and cabbage and walked toward our apartment. After a few minutes, my wife told me what Hilde had said.

"No, she did not say that," I responded. "She's never been very friendly to me."

"Well, that's typical of people here. But she thinks you're sweet!"

Next time I went to Hilde's stall, she greeted me with a big smile. A couple of weeks later, I decided that I would ask her if we could *du* each other. At this point in my German development, I was pretty good at switching between *Sie* and *du*, and I had consistently used *Sie* with Hilde. Although I didn't yet know her name, I asked her, "Can we use "du" with each other?"

"Yes, of course. My name is Hilde."

"And my name is Cooper, like the car Mini Cooper, without the mini."

I frequently said this when I introduced myself. My name is unusual, and some people in Bavaria have a hard time pronouncing "p". It comes out like "b", as in Coober. Sounds a little like Goober, as in goober peas, or sometimes it even sounds like Kuba, Cuba with a K. So I thought it would be easier if I explained my name through something that was familiar to Germans.

My wife must have used my name when Hilde told her how sweet I was. She heard my name as Kurt, which is a more common German name for a man. So, it had stuck with her. After I introduced myself as Cooper, Hilde said,

"So, Kurt, what would you like to buy today?"

I told her that I wanted some turnips and potatoes—I was allowed to pick out my own produce now—and then she asked, "And something else, Kurt?" When we said goodbye, I heard, "Until next time, Kurt."

Over the course of the next year, my name morphed into a nickname, indicating that we were on even friendlier terms: Kurtie. I had a German name, and I could see that I was on my way to becoming German. When I told my wife about the latest development in my friendship with Hilde, she teased that it was time for me to take her last name, Spiegel. Cooper Spiegel sounded awful, but maybe I could live with Kurt Spiegel.

But not Kurtie. Hilde is the only person who is allowed to call me Kurtie.

* * * * *

Through one of my wife's colleagues I heard about a men's discussion group that met regularly in Fürth, a city that borders Nürnberg. I was a founder and member of several men's groups in the U.S.—in the 1970's and 1980's we called them consciousness raising groups. I missed the friendships I had had with men in the U.S. I thought that this group might be a place for me to develop friendships with men here.

I attended a few times and found it interesting, but it pushed the limits of my German. Like in the self-help group I sometimes attended on Wednesday evenings in Nürnberg, there were new voices and sometimes dialects for me to get used to, but it was less structured than the self-help group. That made it more difficult, and I didn't feel much warmth or openness in the group. No one introduced himself to me, and no one asked me any questions. It felt like I had to fend for myself. I felt like an outsider.

I admired these men for coming to this meeting and wanting to talk with other men about their lives and relationships, instead of only talking about work, politics, sports, and hobbies. However, in comparison with the men I knew in the U.S. who attended these kinds of groups, these men talked about personal issues in a way that I didn't recognize. It seemed like they were talking about concepts instead of themselves. I seldom heard anyone talk directly about their feelings.

Sometimes when they talked about their own experiences, the pronoun they used was *one* instead of *I*. It's a little like someone using *you* in spoken English, as in, "You know, when your boss calls you into her office and you worry what you did wrong?" When I hear this, I assume that the person is actually talking about themselves.

When the men in this group used *one*, it sounded to me like they were talking about men as an abstract idea. As a result, I got the impression that they were trying to keep some distance between themselves and the other men in the group. I don't know if this is true, but it sounded like that to me.

When I talked about my experiences, sharing my feelings directly, sometimes passionately, I didn't have a sense that I was seen or heard or understood in this group. I was used to getting a direct response from other men in the groups I had attended in the U.S., but here, no one responded to what I said. Unlike in the self-help group, I didn't get compliments from these men. That led me to think that I had done something inappropriate.

Despite my reservations about the group, I continued to attend. I held onto the idea that I might find a few friends. Of course, I got to practice my German.

One night, Helmut was sitting next to me. I introduced myself to him as if we hadn't met. He responded, "We've already met." I was embarrassed. It happened frequently that I met someone and couldn't remember that we had already met. I don't think it was old age, at least not yet; I think it was something to do with how hard I was working at using German, and because of that, it was too much to remember faces and names. The fact that I was still a little nervous using German undoubtedly had an impact on my memory.

Helmut asked me if I wanted to get together sometime. I agreed, and we met about a week later in a restaurant and talked for a couple of hours. I learned about his work and current relationship, and he was interested in hearing about my experience as an immigrant.

As we were getting ready to leave, he told me, "I am really impressed with you. You moved to Germany in your middle age, you are learning German, you are trying to become part of this culture."

It seemed like the first time that a relative stranger here had so directly noticed my skills and courage. I felt seen by him.

I told him what I had experienced and heard from other immigrants: that we aren't seen, and we don't have a sense that we are valued here. It was new information for him, but he was interested to hear it and didn't get defensive or tell me that the problem was that immigrants don't try to integrate. Since I heard this accusation from other Germans, I was grateful that I didn't hear it from him.

In spite of my ambivalence about the men's discussion group, I occasionally attended over the next couple of years. Slowly, I began to feel a little more comfortable. One night, eight of us were talking about how our roles change as we get older. I was taking part in the conversation, doing my best to share something about my experiences. I was enjoying it.

For some reason, I don't know why, on this night I began to wonder how I sound in German. I'm sure that I sound different as I speak German, in comparison to when I speak English. But what did these men hear? I didn't recognize myself when I spoke German. It sounded strange to me, to hear myself use German, and it seemed especially poignant because I was talking on this night about my identity as a man. I thought, who is this man talking?

I suspect that I will never know the answer to this question, and maybe it is has little to do with language. My perception of myself will probably always be different from what others see in me. In my journal, the next day I wrote, "Using German is an opportunity for me to let go of others' impressions of me and of how I try to impress people. I can't control what others hear when I speak."

When I went to the group the following month, I continued to notice the sound of my voice, and I paid more attention to the sound of the others' voices. Instead of hearing what had been for me a stereotypical German male voice, I heard a rich variety of accents and dialects. I no longer heard the voice of Hitler that I heard when I first came to Germany, and I began to think of these German men as individuals with a wide variety of life experiences.

* * * * *

In German culture, compliments aren't given as much as I am used to, or in a way that I recognize. *Nicht schlecht* (not bad) seems to be a high compliment here. Some Germans have told me that there is a cultural prohibition against complimenting yourself: *Eigenlob stinkt* translates to *praising yourself stinks*.

People from the U.S. have a reputation here of being superficial, and I think there is some truth to that. For example, we give compliments freely and sometimes exaggerate our praise. By German standards, our compliments are not trustworthy.

Since I am conditioned to U.S. standards, I was used to getting more praise. Here, I was feeling a little empty. I was stroke deprived. To make up for this, I gave myself strokes—Cooper, your German is good enough—and I tried to get strokes from other people. Out of habit, I gave strokes to others.

Sometimes people didn't know what to do with my compliments—they had a blank look on their face and said nothing in response—but sometimes I was successful in getting them to give me compliments. If I said, "I'm 57, and I've only been learning German for the last four years, and I haven't really been living here full time," then sometimes they told me that my German was good.

In addition, I was greeting strangers and neighbors, sharing personal information, and asking personal questions. All were violations of unwritten cultural rules in Germany, and I was doing so knowing that I might be seen as a stereotypical American. But sometimes it worked, and we had a conversation.

When I think back about these conversations, I suspect that I was trying to get Germans to recognize me, in addition to finding ways to practice German. In the process of communicating with Germans, I was making decisions about how much I was willing, and able, to adjust to cultural expectations around language. Sometimes I was aware of making these decisions, sometimes not.

For example, in Bavaria, many people say, *Grüß Gott* (greet God) instead of *Guten Tag* (good day) which is common in other parts of Germany. I got into the habit of greeting people with *Grüß Gott* even though I would never say something equivalent in English and even though I don't believe in God. I didn't need to do this—I could have said *Guten Tag* which would have been acceptable. I did not think critically about the decision to use *Grüß Gott*. I just did it.

On the other hand, I was very aware that the German I had learned, and used, was standard German. It isn't the German spoken in everyday conversations. For that, most people use slang or dialect, unless they have high a level of formal education and the setting is formal—like a lecture or public meeting—in which case standard German is typically used.

Although I thought that I was learning standard German, I had also picked up words and phrases from listening to everyday conversations and incorporated them into my vocabulary. I didn't know that I had done that unless someone pointed it out to me. Not surprisingly, I picked up an accent typical of how people in this region speak.

On a vacation in Corsica, I met a Dutch couple. We spoke German together. After a few minutes, they asked, "You come from Bavaria, don't you?"

"Yeah, I live in Bavaria although I come from the U.S. But you can hear that in my voice?"

"Very clearly."

A old friend of mine in the U.S., who lived as a child in Berlin, came to visit me in Germany. I tried to impress him with my German. He teased me: "You don't speak proper German. You sound like someone from southern Germany."

Despite how I sounded, I still spoke more standard German than slang or dialect. When I spoke with the women in the market, my wife's family, the guys I worked with renovating the house in Höfles—I couldn't talk with them in the familiar style that they could use with each other.

Sometimes I wondered if I sounded "snobby" because I used so much standard German. But there was nothing I could do about it, except hope that they would understand my dilemma. In fact, some of them tried to use standard German to accommodate my inability to use their version of German.

Then there was the problem of how to express my feelings in German. I got some feedback from Berndt that the words I used to describe my feelings might not make sense to Germans. So I asked him to coach me. We met at his house one evening, I described the feelings I most wanted to express, and he gave me the vocabulary and phrasing I needed.

If I wanted to say "I am angry" or I am scared," I would translate literally from English to German. But Berndt told me that this would sound too strong for most Germans, who would probably never say, "Ich bin wütend" or "Ich bin ängstlich." They would put it in a context for why they were feeling angry or scared, and they would probably express it in a milder way, for example, "That doesn't please me" instead of "I am angry," and "I'm a little unsure of myself" instead "I am scared."

I decided to try to adjust to German standards. Not in the sense that I would avoid talking about my feelings—they were too important for me to do that. I only wanted to learn how to do this in a way that native German speakers could understand. I wanted to find a way to communicate in German that fit with my sense of myself as a person who was not German. I didn't have the goal of sounding like a native speaker, like some people do, and in any case, I am reasonably sure it isn't possible. I will never sound like a native speaker, not when I began learning German at the age of 53. I just wanted to find a way to express myself in a language that sounds and feels foreign to me.

One day, I was re-reading *Second Language Acquistion* by Rob Ellis. Referring to the work of Bonny Pierce, a Canadian woman who studies SLA, Ellis writes, "Successful learners are those who reflect critically on how they engage with native speakers and who are prepared to challenge the accepted social order by constructing and asserting social identities of their own choice. (page 42)"

That made sense to me. I was making decisions about how I would engage with Germans, and in the process trying to create an identity as an outsider, an identity that would fit me. I was trying to recognize the new person I was becoming.

I don't know if I was, or am, a successful language learner, and I don't know if my attempt to "construct and assert" a new identity had an impact on my ability to learn German. What I do know is that my self-confidence using German grew after I spent nine months renovating our place in Höfles, getting to know some local people, and feeling a part of that small community, even though I was a bit exotic.

One day a friend came to visit us in Höfles and couldn't find the house. She asked a neighbor in the village where house number 21 might be, but since the houses are numbered based on when they were built, not where they are located, no one really remembers house numbers.

So, our neighbor asked her who she was looking for.

"The couple that bought a house here recently."

"Oh, da Ami!" he replied, and pointed out our house.

When she arrived, she told us what had just happened. Not only did local people know who I was and where I lived, I had even acquired a nickname, which in the dialect for this region means, "Der Americaner." The American. Da Ami.

For a couple of years prior to this, I had played with the idea of starting a small business making salad dressing. It was motivated in part by my desire to find something creative and rewarding to do here, and in part by my dislike of the salad dressing I was served in restaurants. I had made my own salad dressing in the U.S. for decades, so I started making it here. My wife and a few of her friends loved it. They encouraged me to start a small business making and selling it.

I bought a case of bottles and found a source for bulk oil and vinegar. I was all set, except I still needed a name for my product. A few weeks after I first heard my nickname in the village, it came to me: "Da Ami in Höfles" would be the brand name for my famous salad dressing.

An immigrant from Argentina I met in Nürnberg loved my salad dressing and thought I needed a more attractive label. So he designed one for me and found a local guy who was willing to print them for practically nothing. Now I had a good product, and was ready to go into production.

A few months later, right before Christmas, I manufactured about 30 bottles. Friends bought bottles to give as Christmas presents, and I gave some away as samples. I made some half-hearted attempts at marketing, but my business didn't grow.

I don't think that was the point, anyway. I was proud of what I had done. I still am. Perhaps the name of my salad dressing—Da Ami in Höfles—was an attempt to bring my two identities together.

One day, I was walking on the outskirts of the village. The smell of the fresh cut hay took me back almost 40 years to a time that I lived on a farm in Good Thunder, Minnesota. Suddenly, I realized that Höfles was not my first experience with German village life. Most of the residents of Good Thunder were descendants of German immigrants.

It was an accident that I ended up in Good Thunder. After college, I had no idea what I wanted to do. The Vietnam War was tearing the country apart, and I was a lost soul. A teacher asked me to come to Minnesota and help create a new graduate program in experiential education, and one of the other students invited me to live with him and his wife and their two-year-old daughter on a farm. I knew something about education but nothing about farming.

Within months of moving there, I felt at home for the first time in my life. I realized the pressure I had been living with growing up on the East Coast: pressure to please my parents and be a good boy, pressure to get good grades in school, pressure to find a career, pressure to find the right way to express my thoughts, pressure to prove my self-worth through words.

In Good Thunder, I was working with my hands and living with the cycles of nature. I learned to milk goats, raise pigs and chickens, grow a garden, build a barn, cut firewood, make my own bread and cheese, and cope with frigid winters and steamy summers. I found a community where it seemed that supporting your family and helping your neighbor were more important than impressing people with what you knew or your status in life.

Of course, there were conflicts between neighbors and fights within families, times that people stopped talking to each other, occasional violence. Yet, it was a radically different life than the one I had had for the first 21 years of my life. When he needed to be gone overnight, my neighbor Mike asked me to feed his pigs, and when my car got stuck in the snow, he was there to pull me out with his tractor.

Slowly I got to know my neighbors in Good Thunder and was invited into their houses for coffee and cake in the afternoon. We all spoke English, and yet our languages were different: at first I tended to use big, complicated words, tried to use proper grammar, and worried if I was saying things exactly as I wanted to. My neighbors tended to use simpler words and expressions, didn't seem to worry about grammar, and seemed more comfortable with silence. There were many things we didn't talk about, or couldn't talk about, or didn't want to talk about. But we found a way to communicate.

Because of my long hair and my beard, and the fact that friends occasionally lived with me on the farm, locals began to refer to us as the hippie commune. Everyone knew who we were, and even though we were exotic, we were accepted as part of the community.

So Höfles was not the first time that I had lived in a German village. Slowly, I began to feel as if I had come back home.

Confrontation

One night at the men's discussion group there was a man about my age who was dominating the conversation and giving unsolicited advice to other men in the group. His behavior was irritating me, but no one else seemed to mind. At least, no one appeared to be irritated like I was, and no one said anything to him. When he again interrupted someone to give them his advice, I impulsively said, with some anger in my voice, "Can't you just listen?"

He got quiet. My comment had the effect I intended. I was glad that he had stopped talking, but I didn't like how impulsive I was and how harsh I sounded. I could have done this more skillfully.

Eventually, I apologized for what I had said, adding that some of the problem was my German. "Things don't come out of my mouth," I told the group, "like I want them to sound. I don't have the ability to be soft in what I want to say. I don't have the vocabulary to do that."

I didn't know how the other men in this group might handle a situation like this. I hadn't seen any conflict, and in my experience with Germans, they tended to avoid conflict in a situation like this. There wasn't any reaction in the group to my anger or my apology: no one criticized me or supported me, publicly or privately.

When I got home and told my wife about what had happened, she confirmed my suspicion. I had violated a cultural norm in a group like this: rarely would someone directly criticize another person in the group as I had done. She thinks that Germans are far too polite and formal to do that.

The following week I happened to see Ulrike, the therapist. I told her about the incident in the men's group, and she complimented me for speaking up and telling the man to stop. In her opinion, people don't do that enough in Germany, with the exception of telling people off when they walk against a red light or ride a bike when they are supposed to walk it. In fact, that happened to me a few weeks later.

I had been singing in a chorus for about a year. A man in the theatre games workshop, who was a long time member of the chorus, encouraged me to join. It was an interesting experience for me, singing with a group of native speaking Germans. Most of the songs were in English or Portuguese, a few were in Bantu, Swahili, Zulu, and French, and we spoke German with each other. We practiced once a week in a school across town and gave concerts a few times a year. Sometimes I enjoyed it, sometimes I found it really challenging.

One evening, as I was going to rehearsal on my bike, I turned left off the main road onto a side road, and a stranger yelled at me for having crossed through a red light. It was hard to know if I had actually violated the law because at this intersection there wasn't a special turn signal for bikes. I tried to explain that to him, and he got aggressive. I wanted to tell him, "Stop it." But I got confused and instead said to him, "Pass auf."

Pass auf means *watch out*. It has two different meanings depending on context. I could use it to warn someone in a situation where I thought they were about to make a mistake and hurt themselves, like running out into the street without first looking. That was how I had used the expression with some children in the neighborhood, and until this point, it was the only meaning I knew.

After I got home, my wife explained to me that in this context *pass auf* meant that I was threatening him, giving him a warning that he better be careful with me. In fact, when I said "Pass auf" to him, he got even more aggressive with me and wanted to have a fist fight. I quickly rode off on my bicycle.

I knew I should ignore men like this. It wasn't the first time that a stranger in Germany had told me off when I was riding my bike and doing something that he thought I shouldn't be doing. It seems a particular obsession with some German men to point out traffic violations to strangers. Maybe I was learning how to confront people, but maybe I needed to learn to pick my battles and be a bit more skilled at how I confronted native German speakers, especially men.

By the time I got to rehearsal, I was still feeling angry. I told a couple of woman in the chorus what had just happened to me. I took it one step further and told them that immigrants aren't welcome here. I used the word *Ausländerfeindlichkeit* (xenophobia or hatred of foreigners) to describe how Germans treat people like me.

In truth, I had no evidence that the guy at the intersection was hostile to foreigners or even if he had said what he did because I'm an immigrant. My experience with him had nothing to do with my experience in the chorus, where I had been welcomed. Also, it clearly had nothing to do with the two women who I was now talking with.

Adding fuel to the fire, the two women disagreed with my perception about German treatment of foreigners. "There isn't any *Ausländerfeindlichkeit* here," one of the women told me. "Maybe Germans are a little private, or maybe a little nervous around strangers, but they are not hostile to foreigners."

The other one added, "I teach in a school where there are immigrant kids. I work hard to help them."

"You are forgetting that it is difficult to be an immigrant here," I responded. "This is a country that doesn't welcome immigrants."

"That's not my fault," replied one of the women. "I am doing what I can, and immigrants need to appreciate that. They also have to try."

"We do! And it takes a lot of energy. We are tired of trying so hard, and some immigrants have given up. You don't understand how hard it is."

"They need to keep trying."

We continued like this for a few more minutes, but I wasn't willing to see the truth in their perception, and they were not willing to see the truth in mine.

Later, I realized that I provoked the conversation with them. Instead of confining my anger to a few individuals who had treated me in a way I didn't like, I was projecting my anger onto German culture and Germans, seeing acts of hostility toward me at every turn, and ready to take on any German who disagreed with me.

For reasons that are still not clear to me, I think that I was recycling back to an earlier stage of being in a foreign culture and using a foreign language. I was again feeling the rage that Eva Hoffman had described. I was again judging German culture and Germans despite the advice my acquaintance in Boston had given me to accept things as they are. Adjusting to living here was taking longer than I expected. I was moving forward a few steps and then falling back. I was going through a phase of regression.

And yet, I believe that expressing my anger as an immigrant was an important thing to do, even if it wasn't very comfortable, and even if I didn't express my anger in the most appropriate way. I think this is true for many immigrants: in the face of an unwelcoming culture, and sometimes hostility, expressing our anger is a way for us to find our voice in this new language and to claim our place.

It makes sense to me that Germans don't like it when we express our anger or blame them for our experience in Germany. Of course, they get defensive. I would, too, if I hadn't learned a different way of responding. Because of my work in the U.S., I was often in situations where women, people of color, and lesbian and gay people told me about their anger at men, white people, and heterosexuals. Instead of getting defensive, I learned to listen and see the truth in what they were saying.

I can't expect Germans not to get defensive, but I do wish that they would ask about, and listen to, our experience. I wish that they would be willing to learn something from us. That happened on occasion, and when it did, I felt I could begin to trust Germans a bit more.

So, in hindsight, I think of these confrontations as successes even though I couldn't express my thoughts and feelings as well as I could in English. I am much more able now to express my anger than I was in the first few years. Now I have more choices in how to express my feelings, including not responding.

*****

I managed to get plenty of opportunities to confront Germans, especially when it came to their belief that Turkish people didn't want to learn German. Sometimes I heard this comment on the back of a compliment about how good my German was. Twice in one week I heard this. The first time, I let it go. The second time I decided to respond.

It was again in a shoe store, but this time, instead of watching Fritz try on shoes, I was picking up some shoes that had been repaired. A week before, when I had dropped them off, I had had a nice conversation with the saleswoman. I appreciated how she had interacted with me. So I complimented her when I returned to the store.

"Thanks for speaking German so clearly and slowly. It's easier for me."

"I come from the north of Germany. When I moved here five years ago, I couldn't understand the dialect spoken here. I felt like an outsider."

"I understand. I come from the U.S., I've only been speaking German for a few years, and sometimes I feel like an outsider, too."

She got the cue, and complimented me. "You speak good German."

"Thanks. I'm trying. It's important to me. I think I should speak German here."

At the moment, I was thinking for some reason about other people from the U.S. who don't learn German. I wanted to distinguish myself from them. Although I had been trying not to compare myself to other people, I slipped every now and then.

She got the first cue, and without meaning to, I just gave her the second cue.

"I think Turkish people should learn German. But they don't want to."

I asked myself, do I want to challenge her? And answered myself. Cooper, you're not in a hurry. Go for it.

So I said to her, "I have heard the same thing from other Germans. But you know, there are many Americans living here who don't learn German. I don't hear complaints about them."

She was listening to me, not getting defensive or arguing with me, so I continued.

"And, for older people like me, it's hard. I can understand why older immigrants don't want to learn German."

I guessed that she was about 50, and so I asked her, "Could you imagine moving to another country and having to learn another language at this time in your life?"

"I couldn't do that. I might take a course to learn some phrases to use when I'm traveling, but moving to another country and having to learn another language? No, I couldn't do that."

"I don't think most people could. So, it's strange to me that I hear this comment about Turkish people not learning German when actually, most of them do learn German."

"I know. My boss is Turkish. He speaks great German."

The contradiction startled me. "Then why do you say that Turkish people don't speak German? It's not true. Your boss speaks German."

"Hm," is all she said.

Then I took another risk. "I think that maybe you have a prejudice against Turkish people."

She paused and said, "Maybe you're right."

"Lately I have been thinking that I am prejudiced against Germans. So maybe we both have some things to learn."

I decided to wrap up our conversation. I had gone as far as I could and wanted. I thanked her for the conversation, paid for my shoes, and left. I felt proud that I had been able to respectfully challenge her on her prejudice toward Turkish people, and I felt glad to have met someone who was willing to admit that she might be prejudiced. I had seldom met people in the U.S. who were willing to admit that.

Even though I was getting more skilled at this, not every German was willing to hear what I had to say. Dagmar, a German woman I had met, asked me to write an essay about my experience here. She wanted to publish a collection of essays written by immigrants. When I asked her what she specifically wanted to hear about my experience, she suggested I respond to the question, "What are my feelings about German culture and German people?" Although Dagmar and I had been using German in our conversations and email, we agreed that I would write this in English and then ask my wife to translate it into German. I was not ready to write something like this in German.

I was glad to be asked. It would give me a chance to put into words some of the feelings I had accumulated in my contact with Germans and German culture. It would be an opportunity to give German readers some information about the experience of immigration. From my perspective, few Germans have authentic contact with immigrants and so they don't know much about us.

I began work right away on the essay and finished it in about a week. I took Dagmar's question about my feelings literally. In the essay, I expressed my fear, sadness, and anger in an honest and personal way, but also respectfully. I was careful not to blame Germans, and included examples of Germans who had been friendly and welcoming and accepting. I included what I liked about Germany. I ended the essay with some comments about what I was learning about myself as I lived here.

My wife translated it, and I emailed it to Dagmar. I felt good about what I had written.

She didn't respond for about a month, so I sent her another email, asking her if she received my essay. She emailed me back, apologized for not writing me sooner, and, without telling me anything she liked about what I had written, she criticized it. She told me in detail that my observations about Germans and Germany were inaccurate, and she disagreed that there is *Ausländerfeindlichkeit* here. Interestingly, I hadn't used this word in my essay. I could have, but I had avoided it because I thought it might be too provocative for German readers.

I felt really discounted by Dagmar's comments. She had asked me to write about my feelings, I did, and then she told me that my feelings were not accurate. This felt crazy to me: my experience is what it is. How could she possibly know what is "true" in my experience? It seemed to reflect what I had often sensed about German culture: that feelings are considered too subjective to be trustworthy. Facts, and the experts who know the facts, are objective. These experts are the sources of truth, not those of us who know the truth of our experience, and who find truth in our feelings.

I wrote her a long email in response, in German, explaining why I felt angry when I read her email. It took me about two hours to write what would have taken me a half hour in English.

I'm sure that some of I wrote was difficult to understand. I was thinking in English, but writing in German. If my German had been better, maybe I could have better explained why I was angry with her.

And I could have asked my wife to edit what I wrote, but I didn't want her to do that. I needed to write this on my own. My anger gave me the energy to find the words that I needed to say.

A couple of weeks later, Dagmar responded to me, still defensively. She didn't understand what I was trying to say. I let it go, and didn't respond further. I was satisfied with how I had tried to express my thoughts and feelings in German.

I told some friends that this seemed to be a turning point for me. I wasn't able to get her to understand my position, but I was able to express my anger respectfully. I was finding my voice and establishing my right to be here.

Holding On

It was a warm summer evening. I was riding my bike home from a chorus rehearsal. My route took me through Gostenhof, a part of town where many immigrants live. European Cup soccer matches were being played all over Europe, and fans were sitting in outdoor cafés, watching the games on television. I stopped at one of the cafés where Greece was playing Sweden. The broadcast was in Greek. Greek flags were hung around the café. I felt the excitement of the Greek fans and sensed how important it must be for them to have a place where they can be with each other and speak their own language.

Since moving here, I had decided that I should not speak English, except with my wife or when I spoke on the phone with friends in the U.S or England. Of course, there were times when I broke the rule, when Germans or other immigrants wanted to speak English with me, but most of the time, I was pretty strict with myself about using German. Foreign language teachers would have probably praised my decision, and I was proud of my perseverance. I am sure it helped me learn German.

My decision, however, also kept me isolated from contact with other native English speakers and the comfort of using my native language. I felt envious, and sad, when I heard the Greek fans celebrating a goal by their team.

In addition to exacerbating my sense of loneliness, my decision to avoid using English was not very functional at times. If my goal was to communicate, it might have been better to use English some of the time. In fact, in the research on second language learning, I read that it is helpful to use your mother tongue from time to time. Maybe if I had told myself that I was using a "well known learning strategy," then I would have had some psychological permission to use English a little bit more.

While doing some consulting work in Frankfurt, I asked a woman from the U.S. about her experience with this—she had been living in Germany for about eight years—and she told me that she frequently used English for the first few years that she was here even as she was learning German. I noticed that she still used English in conversations with German friends and colleagues even as they used German with her. She suggested I negotiate with people about which language to use.

So, I tried this out with a couple of native German speakers in Nürnberg. It probably sounded a little strange to overhear a conversation in two languages, but it worked. I felt more comfortable.

When it came to native English speakers in Nürnberg, I couldn't find any that I really wanted to spend time with. I tried, and it wasn't very satisfying. Most of the people I met were much younger than me and had other interests. They worked for a multinational corporation or were connected to the U.S. military which has large bases nearby.

There were exceptions. At one point, a student in my German class introduced me to a woman from California. She and I had some great conversations. She was the first person from my own country who I really wanted to talk with. It was easy to communicate. We used slang and expressions that only someone from the U.S. would understand.

A year later, she decided to leave Germany and return to the U.S. As I said goodbye to her, I realized that I was going to miss our conversations, even though we had never become really close friends, and I didn't think we would stay in touch. But I had enjoyed the familiarity of speaking English with her.

Sometime later my wife said to me, "I wish that you had some English speaking friends here."

I agreed. I missed the feeling of English words coming easily and quickly out of my mouth.

Around that time, I met a man who lived in London. David and I slowly formed a friendship. I visited him a couple of times, and then he came to Germany to visit me. I felt like he was a brother. We had a lot in common and lots to talk about: our relationships with women and men, our childhood, our neuroses, our work. We talked for hours without a break.

In our conversations I could remember what I know and who I am. I felt at home with him.

* * * * *

Sometimes I used English with other immigrants, because they wanted to practice speaking English, or because their English was better than their German. In some cases, it was the only language we had in common. Regardless of why we used English, I clearly had an advantage: I could use my native language. It didn't feel like work for me to be in the conversation, as I imagined it might be for some people using English as a second language.

In these situations, I tried to speak slowly and clearly, avoiding run on sentences and obscure words. If I spoke English in my "normal" voice like I did with friends from the U.S., or with David, I'm pretty sure others would have felt lost. I had seen this happen with my wife, and I had experienced this with native German speakers when they spoke in their "normal" voice.

So, for example, when I spoke with Mehmet, a young man from Turkey who lived in Nürnberg, I simplified my English. He really appreciated it. Other people also noticed this and thanked me for doing it. I liked speaking this way, too. It gave me time to think about what I really wanted to say instead of just reacting.

On the other hand, I sometimes had the opportunity to use English with non native speakers exactly the way I would use English in the U.S. A German woman asked me one day how we use the word *fuck* in English. I loved her question. There are contexts where I think *fuck* and *fucking* are great words. So, I gave her a short lesson. I exaggerated and used as many variations of *fuck* and *fucking* as I could, pronouncing them just as I would in the U.S. She dutifully repeated everything I said, including laughing with me at the absurdity of our conversation. I hadn't laughed so much in a long time.

My friend Matho and I spoke English the first time we met and continued to do so. Shortly after meeting me, he told me that I should visit India. The next year, I flew to Ladakh, in northeast India, where he met me at the airport. I spent two weeks with him, visiting his home village and his family. My wife couldn't get away from work for the trip and never quite forgave me for having this adventure without her.

A couple of years later, she and I decided to go to South India and asked Matho to come with us. He hadn't spent much time in the southern states, and because he is a tour guide, he was happy to come along with us and get to know that part of his country. We traveled through three states: Tamil Nadu, Karnataka, and Kerala.

In Karnataka, we stayed for three nights in the mountains near Madikeri. There were five of us: me, my wife, Matho, and two women we had met at the guest house, an Indian woman and an Israeli woman. Collectively, we spoke at least 12 languages, but our only common language was English. So that's what we used.

One night we sat around a fire, late into the night, talking about cultural differences, personal goals, romantic relationships, and spirituality—not a light conversation. It was a luxury for me to be able to use my mother language, while the others all had to use a second language.

In many places in the world, I can get by with my native language. I don't need to learn a second language. Everyone in this group, however, needed to learn a second language if they wanted to travel, or work, or live outside their native country.

My friend Francois believes it's actually a disadvantage to grow up in an English speaking country like the U.S. He speaks five languages, which gives him a big advantage in his ability to communicate with a wider range of people. He grew up with the expectation that he would be multi-lingual. As a child and young man, he was always learning a second language. For him, it is not a big deal to learn or use another language.

But it is for me. Like most native English speakers in the U.S., I had to take classes in a foreign language, usually French or Spanish, when I was a teenager. I wasn't expected to actually use this language, except maybe for travel. It was simply required for graduation from High School. No other languages were spoken at home, among my relatives, or in the town where I grew up. There was no model of being multilingual.

* * * * *

When I told people in the U.S. what I was doing—living in Germany and learning German—the response I often got was, "That takes a lot of courage." Sometimes, Germans would nod their heads in a gesture of understanding and simply say, "Respect," meaning, "I have a lot of respect for you."

I rarely felt courageous or had a sense of respect for the decision I had made. Instead, I felt unsure of the decision I had made. I often asked myself, why in the world would I want to learn another language, when I could be sitting back and enjoying life? I am almost 60. Maybe I have 20 years left to live. Is this how I want to spend my time, feeling so stressed out?

There are several things that are important to me at this point in my life. Language learning is only one of them. If I were younger, I could imagine that studying another language, and achieving a high level of fluency, would be important for career goals, and that I would be willing to commit time and energy to achieve this.

Learning German competes with so many other activities: enjoying time with my wife, daily meditation and time in silence, writing, reading, physical exercise, developing a counseling practice, being a member of several groups in Nürnberg including the Integration Council, building and maintaining friendships, renovating our weekend house. I think my German is good enough for the kind of communication that I want and need for a life here.

And as I get older, I have gotten more anxious and insecure and stuck in my ways. Speaking, reading, and writing English are easier for me. I'm not sure how much I want to change, or can change, when it comes to something as basic as language, and my ability to express myself.

So I hold onto English because I don't have that much energy for studying German. I don't want to take classes anymore. I want to express my thoughts and feelings in a language that is familiar.

I notice the change in my wife's behavior on the phone when she's talking to her family in her dialect, Oberpfälzisch. Her voice sounds more relaxed and playful. When she has met someone for the first time and learns that they also grew up in the Oberpfalz, it's the first thing she tells me: "They speak my dialect." She warms up to them immediately and shifts into her dialect even though they might have started the conversation in standard German. For her, speaking dialect is a form of intimacy.

One day she and I listened to a program on Bayern 2. The topic was praying. My wife heard a phrase that really interested her—*gefühle Worten geben*—literally, "to give words to feelings." It could also be translated "to give voice to what is inside us." In the radio program, several people described how they express their inner feelings through prayer and song as a way to cope with helplessness, powerlessness, and suffering.

As immigrants in Germany, we feel some degree of helplessness and powerlessness (some of us more, some of us less), and sometimes we suffer. Of course, we use our native language to try to express what we are feeling. We could try to do it in German, but it probably wouldn't adequately express our feelings. For most of us, it is perhaps only in our native language that we can give voice to what is inside us.

* * * * *

Since we first met, my wife and I have spoken English together. It's our native language as a couple. It's the language we use for everyday conversation and for intimacy. Because her English is really good, I didn't have to learn German to communicate with her. And in fact, I can't imagine feeling intimate with her if we were to use German.

Every once in a while, a well-meaning German told me, "You should speak German at home, with your wife, and then you'd learn more quickly."

That may be true, but I was not willing to use German at home. Home was where I relaxed, where I found comfort, where I spent time with my wife, not where I went for language learning. Two other immigrants I know, both married to German woman, said the same thing. They were learning German, but they wanted to do it outside the house, and they didn't want their wives to be their teachers.

Unfortunately, my wife wanted to be my German teacher. Sometimes she corrected the mistakes I made in German. If I asked for her help with a definition, or grammar, or phrasing, then it felt okay. But if she spontaneously decided to "help" me, I could feel anger rising in my body.

This particular anger felt like the anger of a child and reminded me of how my father wanted to be my teacher. When my wife tried this, I told her, "Stop it. Don't do that." I'm sure that what she was trying to teach me was useful, but I was not able to listen to her. I wanted her to be my partner and lover. I didn't want her to be my teacher.

It's not like I didn't need my wife. I did. I still do. I am very dependent on her.

When I first moved here, it was painful for me to realize how dependent I was. I wanted to think that I could be independent. But slowly I have accepted and even appreciated the value of being dependent on someone. I have come to realize that it was a delusion to think that I was independent. I am dependent on so many people for so many things.

At the same time, the longer I live here, I am less dependent on her as my personal translator. There are a variety of people I ask when I don't understand something about the language or the culture.

And, curiously, I am less rigid about only using English with her. Sometimes I use German at home: I write her notes in German, we discuss plans and talk about superficial things in German, and when we visit her family or when we get together with German friends, she and I almost always use German with each other. It wouldn't feel comfortable for me to use English when everyone else is using German, especially around my wife's family, who don't understand English.

Maybe there will be a time in the future when we use German more than we use English, even for sharing our feelings. If that happens, I suspect that I will see another side of my wife. We will probably never use the language in which she finds her core identity—Oberpfälzisch—but I am sure it would be different for her if she regularly used standard German with me. I also suspect that it would change our relationship. I don't know how it would change, but I think it would.

At a week-long seminar in France, I had several opportunities to experience how our choice of language impacts us and our relationships. We were a multinational group with only two native English speakers. The other participants' fluency in English ranged from high to low. But the working language was English, because it was the only language we had in common and because two of the three facilitators only spoke English.

Early in the seminar, a few participants occasionally used their native language with someone from their own country. When this happened, the facilitators immediately requested a translation. They seemed uncomfortable with not understanding what the participants were saying.

I suspect that we made an unconscious collective decision to use English, to take care of the facilitators, even though we never formally agreed to do so. The seminar was advertised as being in English, and yet we could have decided to be multi-lingual. We could have developed a guideline that anyone could use their native language whenever they wanted to. But we didn't. The facilitators didn't suggest that, and neither did we.

On the last day, a Dutch participant decided to confront the facilitators. She had privately expressed her frustration with the program but had not yet felt comfortable saying that to the facilitators. She didn't feel confident speaking English, especially since what she wanted to say would not be pleasant. So she had been hesitant to say anything publicly, even though she wanted to.

She gathered her courage and told the facilitators what she was feeling and thinking. And, not surprisingly, she stumbled over her words and minimized her criticism. Her voice was small. The facilitators listened to her but didn't hear her. I thought to myself, "I wish that she had said this in Dutch." I had heard her using Dutch with another participant in the seminar, and I knew how powerful she could be.

On the next break, I approached her, congratulated her, and asked her how she was feeling.

"I lost my confidence when I had to speak English. I didn't say what I wanted to. And they didn't understand."

"I know."

"I could have said it better in Dutch. I could have asked Eva, who speaks really good English, and she could have translated for me."

Later, over dinner, I was sitting with her and two other Dutch women. Collectively, they spoke at least five languages, but we were speaking English together. So, I asked them, "Why are we speaking English?"

"Oh, probably because it's the one language we have in common. And probably to accommodate you."

"But we don't have to use English. What if we each use the language we want to?"

They all agreed, and the dinner conversation took on a completely different character. The four of us switched in and out of English, Hebrew, German, Dutch, and French. It was a much more playful and lively conversation. We didn't always understand each other's words, but we felt very connected to each other. Each person seemed more confident using the language that they chose to use, instead of having to use English.

I experimented with using German and French during dinner. I could express myself reasonably well in German, but my French had really deteriorated since I had started learning and using German, so I wasn't able to express my thoughts very well in French. I avoided using English for most of the conversation.

At one point, one of the women told me, in English, "Cooper, I feel that our relationship is more balanced when you use German or French. Then we are both using a second language, and I'm not at a disadvantage."

*****

In the fall of 2009, I attended a daylong forum on human rights in Nürnberg. As a result of Nürnberg's history as the site of the annual Nazi party rallies in the 1930's and the site of the Nürnberg Trials after the war, human rights take on a particular importance here. In a morning plenary, we heard from a prosecutor at the International Court and then heard reports from international representatives of the Coalition of European Cities against Racism. Each of them told us about the work of their city in combating racism.

The forum took place in an auditorium on the second floor in the old city hall. It felt like I was a part of history, sitting in a 300-year-old building, knowing that the Nazis marched on the street below during their annual rallies, and now witnessing human rights advocacy. The guest speaker and seven invited representatives were seated at an oval table at the front of the room. Translators were working in the glass booth at the rear corner of the auditorium. We each had a headset and a microphone at our seat and could choose if we wanted to listen to the speakers in English or German.

Herr A. gave a report about what Nürnberg had done as a member of the Coalition. He was the head of the office that responds to allegations of discrimination. I was familiar with this kind of work; in Cambridge, Massachusetts, I was a member of the Human Rights Commission, where we monitored discrimination, responded to complaints, and mediated cases.

A soft spoken Black man in the audience, speaking in formal, polite German, had a question for Herr A. He wanted to know what Herr A.'s office was doing specifically to address racism faced by people of African descent living in Nürnberg.

Herr A.'s response was, in my opinion, defensive and aggressive. He described how hard he had tried to fight discrimination, telling us in detail about one incident where he helped two *farbige Mädchen* (literally, "colored girls" but they are young Black German women) who had been denied admission to a fitness center. He then went on to say that he couldn't do anything if African immigrants didn't bring their complaints to his office, and described how he had tried to get Africans to come to his office and meet with him, without success. He repeated this last point for emphasis. The message was clear: he was doing everything he could, and African immigrants weren't doing enough, to challenge racism.

I was stunned. I expected him to engage in a dialogue with the Black man who had asked the question instead of defending his own actions and blaming

African immigrants. In my work in the U.S., I had often challenged white men like him in positions of authority. Here was an opportunity to use what I had learned and practiced for 30 years, but I didn't know what to say here, in this context.

As if to give me a chance to collect my thoughts, a white middle aged woman raised her hand, was recognized, and turned on her microphone. She told us that she was born and raised in Nürnberg, lived for several years in the U.S., and had now returned home. Then she said how proud she was to be from Nürnberg, where there is a commitment to challenge discrimination and a man like Herr A. to carry out that work. Another member of the audience shared a similar sentiment.

Then I raised my hand, was recognized by Herr A., turned on the microphone at my seat, and started to speak—in English. I introduced myself, said that I was nervous about speaking, but felt a need to say something. In a respectful and soft tone of voice, I told Herr A. and the audience that this was the second time in two months that I had heard people of African descent raise concerns about their experience in Germany, and both times white Germans got defensive and responded as if they were the experts on racism and African immigrants. I told him that his response to the Black German man in the audience was not helpful and likely to increase distrust in him and his office.

I decided to let the comment about "colored girls" go, because it would be too complicated to explain, and I hadn't seen much recognition in Germany that this term is offensive. If I had tried to explain that, I believe that some Germans in the audience might have thought that I was being petty, or inappropriately applying U.S. standards to Germany, and then discount the rest of what I was saying.

I paused. Herr A. then asked me if I could be more concrete in my comments about what he had done that was not helpful. I thanked him for asking me, and I decided to be direct with him. "In my opinion, you were aggressive in your response to the Black German man who asked the question. You blamed him and other Africans living in Nürnberg for not coming to see you, instead of thinking about what you might need to do differently. You could have asked him for suggestions about what you could do differently so that he and others would be more willing to meet with you. You defended your work and the work of the Office of Human Rights. In my experience, that is not listening and hearing, but speaking from a position of power and authority." I heard a few people applauding.

He then switched to German and said, "Perhaps what you hear in my voice is my passion for this work."

I responded in German, "I believe that you are a passionate man and that you care about human rights. But the way you spoke here, when then this man asked his question, was in my opinion, aggressive and disrespectful."

Herr A. did not respond further. Our conversation was over. I had said what I needed to say, in fact, maybe more than I intended. There were a few more comments, and then we took a break.

A man sitting behind me introduced himself and told me in German that he is an acquaintance of Herr A.'s, agrees with what I said, and plans to speak with him about his behavior. I thanked him and told him how important it is that Herr A. get this feedback from Germans like him.

The Black man in the audience who had originally asked Herr A. about racism in Nürnberg approached me. We introduced ourselves and spoke German. Samuel thanked me for my comments.

"You were able to tell Herr A. what I couldn't. Because you are a white man, I think he was willing to listen to you."

"I think that's true. I wish there were someone else who was responsible for this work in Nürnberg, who would listen to you instead of having to hear this from me."

I was very aware that I was using my privilege as a white American to confront Herr A. I believe that what Samuel said was true: many white Germans will listen to me but discount the same words coming from an African immigrant.

I was also aware that using my first language gave me confidence to say exactly want I wanted to say, and in the tone I wanted. When I was speaking with the microphone, I could hear the power in my voice. I had everyone's attention.

But if I had tried to do this in German, there is a possibility that Germans would have discounted what I had said. They would have put me in the category "immigrant" with all of the stereotypes they attach to that.

Using English, I believe I was able to present myself as an "educated" American. In my experience, Germans usually listen to Americans. People who seem "educated"—meaning they have gone to a university—are more likely to be treated as "experts." I am putting all of these words in quotes because I don't believe that I am more of an expert or better educated than, say, African immigrants here—actually I know much less than they do about how racism manifests itself here and impacts their lives—but I am treated as if I am a "superior immigrant."

When I came home and told my wife about this, she said, "Cooper, when you speak in English, you sound more powerful and more gentle. You are yourself. People take you seriously. When you speak German, sometimes you sound harsh, even aggressive. Or you don't sound as confident. People don't take you seriously."

I think my wife is wise, and I usually take her suggestions seriously. Not always, but usually. A couple of weeks later, I had an opportunity to practice her advice. I went to a bakery and asked for a loaf of bread. An older man came in right after me and must have heard the accent in my German that identified me as a native English speaker.

He asked me, in English, "Do you know a pretty woman who could teach me English? I would like to spend some time with a pretty woman."

I paused, and then gently but firmly said, in English, "No, I don't know any."

My first impression of him was not positive. It felt like he was using a style of communicating that I have heard other men use with each other when they talk about women. He had asked for help finding a teacher when he actually wanted a date, maybe sex. I was a perfect stranger, and he was asking me to help him find a woman. It seemed a little sleazy to me. I wouldn't give him the name of any woman I know.

Despite my response, he tried again. "Are you sure? I want to find a pretty woman who will go out with me and speak English with me, you know, an evening in a restaurant together."

I repeated myself, this time more firmly. "I can't help you find a woman."

He must have heard the tone in my voice, because he responded defensively. "Oh, it was only a joke."

"I don't think it was a joke. It wasn't funny."

This time he didn't respond, and I walked out the door.

Silence

As I was renovating the house in Höfles, I spent a lot of time alone. I woke up at 5 a.m. when I heard birds singing, and I worked outside most of the day until nightfall. Then I sat quietly, maybe read a little bit, or simply listened to the sounds of the evening.

This experience was familiar to me. As a child, I spent lots of time alone: playing, reading, building things. As an adult, I need some time in silence every day, sometimes for longer periods. I thrive in silent meditation retreats. So it was wonderful to have time for myself in the peace and quiet of a village in Bavaria.

At the same time, I worried that my German was slipping. I wasn't having conversations, except with myself. I wasn't reading German while I was in Höfles, and I wasn't listening to the radio because I wanted to be surrounded by the sounds coming from the fields and the woods.

Somewhere I read that silence and reflection are important components of second language acquisition. It helps us consolidate what we are learning. If this is true, then it seems like a paradox: my preferred style of learning German has been through social contact.

Occasionally I was told by someone who knows me and has watched my progress in German, that I had really improved. I usually didn't recognize my improvement. This stage of language learning was different from when I was a beginner, when I progressed quickly. Now, the learning curve was relatively flat, but maybe my brain was processing all that I have learned, and slowly I was developing the ability to use this language naturally.

It was definitely a slow process. Even with the improvement that others saw, and that I assumed was happening, there were times when I couldn't find the words in German to express my feelings and thoughts. I had a clear sense of what I was feeling and thinking, and I could even visualize it, but I couldn't express it through words.

As I was writing this book, I was haunted by a distant memory of something I had read in the 1960's in a book by Thomas Wolfe. I couldn't remember the details—I couldn't even remember the name of the novel—but I remembered that it had something to do with the pain of an infant's experience with language. I remembered that when I read this novel as a teenager, I recognized this pain immediately.

So I went to a small English library at the German American Institute in Nürnberg to see if I could possibly find it. I wasn't optimistic, but miraculously, they had an old copy of *Look Homeward Angel,* and I found the passage right away.

> He was caught in agony because he was poverty-stricken in symbols: his mind was caught in a net because he had no words to work with. He had not even names for the objects around him: he probably defined them for himself by some jargon, reinforced by some mangling of the speech that roared around him, to which he listened intently day after day ...
>
> He saw that the great figures that came and went about him, the huge leering heads that bent hideously into his crib, the great voices that rolled incoherently above him, had for one another not much greater understanding that they had for him: that even their speech, their entire fluidity and ease of movement were but meager communicants of their thought or feeling, and served often not to promote understanding, but to deepen and widen strife, bitterness, and prejudice.
>
> His brain went black with terror. He saw himself an inarticulate stranger, an amusing little clown, to be dandled and nursed by these enormous and remote figures. He had been sent from one mystery into another: somewhere within or without his consciousness he heard a great bell ringing faintly, as if it sounded undersea, and as he listened, the ghost of memory walked through his mind, and for a moment he felt that he had almost recovered what he had lost. (p. 36-37)

I realized that my experience of not being able to find the right words was not new. It happens in the language I've known for 60 years. So I think it's a trap for me to think that I will be able to say what I want to say in German if I achieve a certain level of fluency.

I have also experienced situations in which things turned out better because I wasn't able to say what I wanted to say. A German acquaintance invited me to his house for a Sunday brunch with his extended family. While we were sitting at the table and eating, his father-in-law began to preach about the superiority of his Christian faith and insisted that his interpretation of the bible was right and other interpretations were wrong. I wanted to challenge him, not about biblical interpretation, but about his perspective about "right" and "wrong" spiritual practice. I tried and couldn't find the words to explain what I wanted to say.

I eventually said to him, "I don't want to continue this conversation. I don't think we are communicating with each other. I think it's better for us to talk about something else." Not being able to express myself in German allowed me to use a strategy which I almost never use in English: to gently and politely end the conversation instead of trying to get someone to understand my perspective.

There is a concept in Buddhism called "wise speech." It means using language in a way that will be productive and helpful, rather than destructive and hurtful. Wise speech requires thoughtfulness, or like my mother use to say, "Think before you open your mouth."

A few years ago, I saw a video of Suzuki Roshi, a Zen master, giving a talk in English. He spoke slowly, he made mistakes in grammar, his vocabulary was limited, and his Japanese accent was strong, but he was incredibly articulate. He was able to express complex ideas using simple words. Not only was I impressed with his wisdom, by watching him I learned that it might be possible for me to express my own thoughts and feelings in German, even when I might think that my German is not good enough.

Similar to the experience I had in Denver with Robert—where I learned that it was possible to listen to someone without understanding their words—I carry this image of Suzuki Roshi with me. He reminds me that using a second language is an opportunity for me to practice wise speech. I need some extra time to find the words I want to use. It's not automatic and mindless like when I use my first language. But I can express myself in German, if I am patient with myself, and if my listeners are patient with me.

Using German has also helped me better understand how communication is based on much more than words. Before I started learning German, I knew that words are actually a small part of communication: more is actually communicated through gestures, facial expressions, chemicals released from our bodies, and the energy that we sense as emotions in another person.

Yet words are emphasized in language learning, as if we will be able to communicate with someone when we both know the same vocabulary and structure for how to arrange words in a sentence. Knowing that certainly helps communication, but it isn't the only factor.

In the fall of 2009 I went to Budapest to attend a European conference on Human Rights. The working languages were Russian, French, and English; there were translators constantly at work. During a very passionate speech by a Russian activist, I noticed that the translator was also very passionate as he translated into English what the activist was saying in Russian about challenging authority. The translator's tone of voice and the pace of speaking matched the voice of the Russian man. In turn, the audience responded with an enthusiasm that I didn't see at any other time in the conference. If the speaker's intent was to inspire us, I believe he succeeded because of *how* he delivered his comments, and *how* that was translated.

At a coffee break, I found the translator and told him that I appreciated what he had done, that it seemed to me he was emotionally involved with the translation. He responded, "I believe that our job is to translate emotions as well as thoughts. It's not possible to translate word for word between Russian to English—they are different languages with different values and meanings imbedded in the language—but I think it is possible to convey the sense of what someone is saying, and that means I have to try to communicate what the person is feeling."

Long before we bought the house in Höfles, my brother-in-law Peter occasionally asked me to help him with projects at his house. I would take an early morning train to a station near their village, and then Peter or his wife Johanna would pick me up. Because I was in the early stages of learning German, I was nervous. I didn't know how I would be able to communicate with Peter. He could speak some English, but I was committed to using German with him, and I didn't have the vocabulary yet for tools and materials and construction techniques.

But I was also pleased that he had asked me to help him. It gave me an opportunity to pay him back for his generosity with my wife and me. He had helped us move to a new apartment, repaired things for us, and lent me tools and his car. Since I felt confident working with my hands, this would be an opportunity for me to remember what I could do, instead of being reminded that I couldn't communicate very well in German.

We took down an old shed next to his house, and then a few weeks later built a new carport. We cut firewood and burned brush. We broke though a wall and installed a steel beam over a doorway in his basement.

When we worked together, we didn't talk much. We communicated more through gestures than words. Working side by side, in silence, we supported each other. At the end of the day, my body was tired, I felt satisfied, and we had accomplished a lot together.

As I was writing this chapter, and talking with my wife about the overemphasis of words in language, she said to me, "You have an emotional and physical relationship with my mother. You don't have a cognitive relationship. You visit her, and you hug her; she mends your socks, and she cooks you *Schnitzel*."

The currency of my relationship with Anna, like with Peter, is a kind of gift giving. My own mother taught me how to darn my socks, so I can do that for myself, but Anna likes doing that for me. I go see her once in a while. Our conversation doesn't last very long, but she appreciates it. Of course, I thank her for my socks and her food.

Anna is a woman of few words. Although she likes to meet people who live in other villages or different worlds than she does, she is more interested in working in the fields or being in the barn than sitting down and talking. In her world, there is always work to be done. But one time she said to my wife, "My relationship with Cooper is a very special one." And when my wife goes by herself to visit her mother, Anna always asks her, "Where is Cooper? Why didn't he come?"

Ups and Downs

Although I was proud of what I had accomplished, there were times when I felt completely demoralized, when I thought, "I cannot learn and use this language."

One of my teachers asked me to write a recommendation for a web site she was developing. I was happy to. She wanted it in English and German, so I wrote it first in English and then translated it into German. Writing the recommendation in English was easy, but it took me over two hours to translate it. I tried to use a couple of things grammatically that I usually wouldn't: a past tense that is normally used only in written German, a structure for clauses, and some words that I had been trying to learn. When I finished translating it, I felt good about it.

Then I asked my wife to edit it for me, and I anticipated that there would be a few minor corrections. Instead, she completely rewrote it according to how she would say it. My first look at the "edited" version was a page of red marks: she had crossed out and rewritten about 90% of what I had written.

I lost my temper and got angry with her. Actually, I felt hurt. My wife's editing touched a very vulnerable part of me: my belief that I can't express myself in this language.

Sometimes it was hard for me to remember that I was able to express myself in German, not perfectly, but enough to be understood, assuming that someone wanted to understand me. It was also hard for me to remember that learning German is a process. I used to think that learning a second language was a little like cooking a casserole: you find the ingredients, put everything together, pop in the oven, wait a little bit, and then it's finished and you can enjoy it. I thought there would be a point when I would say, "it's done."

But it's never really done. I will never be finished. There will always be more to learn.

It's a little like being a pilgrim on the Camino de Santiago de Compostela. The destination is Santiago, in northwest Spain. But actually, the journey itself is more important than reaching Santiago. In a German guide book to the Camino, pilgrims are reminded, "Der Weg ist das Ziel" (the path is the goal).

Sometimes I didn't quite know where I was going. At one point in 2007, I wrote in my journal, "I seem to be on a plateau right now. I don't have any specific goals." I talked with a couple of people who had clearer goals than I did: One needed to pass a language test to qualify for a permanent visa in stay in Germany, and another, a relative beginner at German, wanted to learn some basic rules of grammar.

It was hard for me to pin down what I wanted to learn, what I wanted to improve. I could only say it in vague terms, like "improve my speaking ability." At those times, it was helpful to remind myself that I was on a journey.

* * * * *

In 2009, on a sunny and warm summer day, I was sitting in a train on my way to Duisburg, a city four hours north of Nürnberg. I was going to a two day meeting with some people who do the same kind of work I did in the U.S. I had met most of them when they were participants in a workshop I led in Frankfurt in 2007. I was excited to see them again and also nervous: this was the first time in Germany that I would be meeting with people who I considered colleagues. We would be discussing how we might collaborate.

I had told them that I would like to present some material about racism in the U.S. that I thought would be helpful in explaining some aspects of racism in Europe. I had presented this material hundreds of times in the U.S., in English, but never in German. As I sat on the train, I rehearsed what I wanted to say. Fortunately, there were not many people on the train, and I found a seat in an empty compartment.

I arrived in Duisburg, and Günter picked me up. He and I had met several times in the past and really liked and trusted each other. I considered him both a friend and colleague. We switched constantly between English and German as we shared news about our lives.

At Günter's house, we met up with Jana, who was a participant in the workshop I had led. She and I went shopping for food. The two of us had taken responsibility for planning meals for the group; it was something we both enjoy doing, and I felt very comfortable with her.

As we shopped, she and I quickly and creatively figured out a menu for the next two days. We only spoke German with each other. In the parking lot, as we were packing up groceries in the car, she said to me, "Your German has improved so much. I am really impressed."

"Really? I don't sense that."

"Yes," she says, "without a question."

Eventually, the others arrived at Günter's house, and we started the meeting with long introductions, since we didn't all know each other. The group included a Dutch-German-Turkish woman, a German-Turkish woman, a French-German woman, four Germans, a Black German woman, and me.

One of the themes in our introductions was language. For example, the Dutch-German-Turkish woman, who was raised in Germany and now lives in Holland, speaks Turkish, German, Dutch, and English. She told us how her choice of language depends on the context and her personal feelings about each language. As I listened to her and the others share their experiences, I was aware of how normal it is for people here to know and use two or more languages, and they have to regularly make decisions about how and when to use each language.

The diversity of the group reminded me of similar experiences I had had in the U.S. The diversity in this group was different than the diversity I experienced in the U.S., but the process felt similar. So, I felt comfortable here.

At the same time I didn't feel completely at home in the group. I think it was probably due to language. I didn't have the ability to tell the group about myself, in German, in a way that I could have said it in English, if I were meeting with colleagues in the U.S. I had to simplify what I said, instead of being able to share complex and subtle aspects of my identity similar to what my colleagues here had done. I think I simply needed more time than the others did to find my voice in this group.

I don't think my discomfort was a question of comprehension: I understood about 95% of what people in the group were saying. Even if I didn't understand, I was able to relax and trust that I would understand sooner or later, or maybe not. I didn't worry about it or get frustrated like I used to.

At 10 p.m., I was really tired. The group wanted to keep meeting; Lena, the Black German woman, had recently written a book about her experiences with racism in Germany and wanted to read some selections. As much as I wanted to hear her and support her, I felt like I needed to be alone and get some sleep. I had been using German continuously for ten hours. It was enough.

The next morning, after a good sleep, I felt more confident and comfortable and talked more than I did the day before. During the day, I had several interesting conversations over breaks and shared some of my thoughts about diversity with the whole group.

Although I didn't give the presentation I had prepared on the train—there wasn't enough time—I did make a couple of observations and suggestions about how we were working together as a group. I wasn't facilitating this group, and yet I was providing some leadership for the group. I was both surprised and proud that I could do this in German.

In the evening, after we said our goodbyes and most of the group had left, I had a long and intense and enjoyable conversation with Lena at Günter's kitchen table. I didn't go to bed until 11pm, and when I realized how late it was, I shook my head in amazement. I had been using German for 14 hours.

I left Günter's house early to catch a train back to Nürnberg. As I was sitting on the train, I got a text message from Lena. She wrote, "Weißt du Cooper, unser Gespräch gestern war für mich das interessanteste, spanneste, schönste, und berührenste dieser zwei Tage. Ich danke dafür." (You know, Cooper, our conversation yesterday was for me the most interesting, exciting, nicest and most touching conversation during the last two days. Thank you for that.)

I saved the message. I wanted to be able to remind myself of what is possible.

I needed to be back in Nürnberg on Saturday afternoon to rehearse with the chorus for a concert on Sunday evening. As I arrived at our rehearsal, people greeted me and asked me how I was doing. I suddenly felt very insecure about using German.

We began to practice the songs we would be performing. I was surrounded by 60 Germans, packed together on a stage that was too small for such a large group. I lost my voice completely and couldn't sing. I sensed that I had to get off the stage immediately. It was similar to panic attacks that I have had a few times in my life. I focused on my breathing and reminded myself that I was okay.

We took a break. I found two men who I liked and trusted, and who I thought might understand what I was experiencing. Although I wasn't sure what had brought on the panic attack, I gave them the best explanation I could: that I felt overwhelmed as the only non-German in such a large group of Germans. The two men listened and understood. They didn't get defensive. When I told them that I might not come to the concert the next day, they told me that they would miss me, and at the same time, they would support my decision.

I slept on it, and the next day I called them and told them that I would not be coming. I asked them to tell the others that I wasn't feeling well. I didn't want the others to hear second hand that I felt overwhelmed by them. I told my two friends that I was grateful for their reaction to my decision. It increased my sense of trust in them, and I felt sad that I would not be singing with them in the concert.

I had no regrets about my decision. It was, and still is sometimes, important for me to set limits on the amount of contact I have with Germans. In the U.S., I often heard women, people of color, lesbian and gay people, and other marginalized groups say that they sometimes need to avoid contact with the dominant group and seek refuge with people in their own group. I, too, have found that it feels more comfortable sometimes to be in the company of other immigrants, even if there are profound cultural differences between us. There is a sense of psychological safety in our shared experience as foreigners in Germany.

Although official Integration policy rejects ghetto-building (which is how the creation of separate communities is described here, and which I find is a misuse of the term *ghetto*), I believe it is essential that we create a space for ourselves, where we find the energy to live in the dominant society. It sounds like we are choosing to live apart from German society, but actually, I think it is one way that we find our place in this society.

My wife and I decided to spend the day hiking. I told her about the experience with my colleagues in Duisburg. I told her about the experience with the chorus. It felt great to use English, and to be with someone I know and trust, even though she is German.

* * * * *

An acquaintance who was a member of a men's support group asked me if I was interested in joining his group. They had been meeting weekly for years and were looking for a couple of new members. I missed the experience of the support groups I had known in the U.S., where we really got to know each other, shared intimate aspects of our lives, and supported each other. So, I told him I was interested, and he invited me to come to their next meeting to see if I wanted to join them and if they wanted me as a member.

I was pleased to be asked. However, at my first meeting, I was very aware that I was the only non-German in the group. Because some of them spoke quickly or in dialect, I had to work pretty hard to follow the conversation. There was also a way that they communicated which I recognized from my experience with other men, both here and in the U.S., but which I didn't like. They didn't seem to be speaking to each other, but speaking to a topic. It didn't feel like a conversation to me, but rather a series of statements. It didn't feel personal.

Although I was pretty sure that group was not what I was looking for, I agreed to come a second time. As I walked to the meeting, I decided to tell them that I wouldn't be joining. I wanted to be honest with them, and I was also a little nervous. I didn't want to imply that there was something wrong with them; in fact, I admired them for their commitment to each other and to learning about themselves as men. I simply wanted to tell them that this group was not for me. I wondered if I would be able to do this in German: be honest about my own thoughts and feelings without offending them.

There was a "check-in" round at the beginning of the meeting. In addition to telling them how I was doing in general, I took a breath and told them, "I've decided that I don't want to join the group. I don't think this is what I am looking for."

One of the men asked me in what I heard as a sharp voice, "How can you make that decision after meeting with us for just one time?"

His question sounded more like an accusation than a question, but I responded as if it were only a request for information.

"I am the only foreigner here. That's difficult for me. I sense how different I am from you. I am sure there are many similarities, but I don't feel like I belong here. I don't feel comfortable as the only foreigner here."

Another man said, "You're not that different from us. U.S. culture and German culture are similar. You've been here a few years now, and you're getting used to this culture."

Even though he had discounted what I had said, there was more than a grain of truth in his comment. Germany is similar to the U.S., and I was getting used to the culture. In fact, my wife teased me from time to time about becoming German. I could see that myself. So, what he had said was in some ways accurate.

What he didn't know is that I react strongly when people challenge me on the validity of my feelings. He might as well have said, "I know more about your personal experience than you do."

I wanted to recognize the validity of what he had said, and at the same time, I wanted to challenge his discount, so I said to him, "You're right. There are similarities between the U.S. and Germany and slowly I am adapting to German culture. But I am still a foreigner. I am not German. I am not the same as you. I am different. I am offended that you can't accept the way I am different."

He answered, "You misunderstood me."

"Maybe I did. That is always a possibility when I am using German. But it is important for me to tell you that I didn't like your comment."

There was a pause, and then another man said, "I don't understand. You seem similar to us. Last meeting it seemed easy for you to be in this group."

"Yes, in some ways. I have been in lot of men's groups. This is familiar to me, and this group is similar to other groups I have been in. What's different is being the only foreigner. If there were more foreigners, I think that it would feel more comfortable for me. I believe that they would understand what I am talking about, and I wouldn't feel so alone."

A couple of the men responded, and it seemed to me that they didn't understand what I was trying to say. So I tried a different approach.

"It's not just being a foreigner. Using German is difficult for me. It takes lots of energy to listen and to speak in German, especially when we are talking about personal things."

"But you're German is so good."

"Sometimes yes, sometimes no. But some of you are speaking dialect, and some of you speak fast, and I don't always understand. I don't want to constantly interrupt, to ask you to repeat or explain things, and I don't want to change the way that you speak with each other. It's important that you speak the way you want to. That means that it is harder for me to be in this group."

There was another pause. Finally, one of the men said, "It sounds like you're pretty sure that you don't want to join this group."

"Yes," I answered. I didn't tell them that I was even more convinced now, based on the way that they had just responded to me.

"I feel disappointed," said another man. "I think that there is a lot that we could learn from you about your experience here in Germany as a foreigner."

"Maybe. If you want to know about that, I could imagine coming here sometime and telling you about that. But it's too much work for me to be a member of this group, and the only foreigner in this group, and use German, and teach you about my experience."

I was aware in this moment, talking to them, that I was simplifying what I was saying because I couldn't articulate in German all that I was thinking. If I had been using English, it might have sounded more like this: "I am making moment by moment decisions about what to say and what not to say, based on what I am capable of saying in German and based on what I think you will understand about my experience as an outsider. I am processing my experience in this group at several layers simultaneously: what I am feeling and thinking about being with you, what I am noticing in the group process here, what I am sensing are cultural differences between us. It is simply more work that I am willing to do in a group where I just want to feel like I belong."

Although I heard and experienced their comments and questions as criticism rather than support, I believe that some of them, maybe all of them, were truly disappointed that I didn't want to be in their group. Later, as we said goodbye, one of the men walked out with me and said, "I didn't realize it was extra work for you to use German. I am glad you explained that."

When I heard that, I felt my trust in him grow and told him, "I look forward to seeing you again. I hope we can spend some time together." I meant it.

As I think about my short experience with this men's group, I am reminded again that most native German speakers didn't know how to adjust their style of speaking when they were communicating with me.

There were exceptions, like Johanna and Peter. They both talked slower and used standard German instead of dialect when they spoke with me. They told their sons Jakob and Sebastian to do that, too. I really appreciated how they recognized my limitations.

Other members of my wife's family, like Barbara, my wife's aunt, also knew how to talk with me. As a young woman, she worked in a factory with many immigrants. So instead of the dialect she spoke with my wife, she used standard German, spoke slowly, and repeated herself when she spoke with me. I was able to have telephone conversations with her when I was still at a beginner level of German. She was the first person here with whom I could comfortably talk on the phone.

She doesn't slow down or repeat herself now although she generally uses standard German with me. Now and again, she uses some dialect, and I use a little bit of dialect with her.

* * * * *

My wife heard about an educational trip to Poland and asked me to come with her. She told me it would be a week-long trip with a focus on the old and complicated relationship between Germany and Poland. We would be visiting

Auschwitz as well as learning about German resistance to the Nazis. I had visited other concentration camps in Germany, and wanted to visit Auschwitz, even though I knew it would be painful. I knew practically nothing about the history of Poland. So, I decided to go.

In November 2009, after a long bus ride, 25 of us arrived in Poland in the evening. The next day, after breakfast, the official program started. Rather than beginning with a group introduction, which I expected, the first day began and ended with lectures. They were quite formal and often consisted of a paper, read by the author, and then a question and answer period. From my perspective, it was very academic and intellectual, and, of course, everything was in German.

I dislike this style of teaching, even in English, and have avoided situations like this since I graduated from college in 1971. Sitting and listening to so-called experts is not generally the way I learn. I learn through experience and reflection on my experience. In my opinion, academic papers are not meant to be read aloud, and it is especially difficult for me to understand this type of formal, written German when it is spoken.

The second day was similar to the first, and by the afternoon, I was exhausted. Not only had I been concentrating as I tried to understand the lectures, but we ate meals with the group in noisy dining halls where it was difficult for me to hear individual conversations. I was grateful that my wife was on the trip, so that we could share our experiences with each other, in English. There was so much for us to talk about. My wife has a learning style that is similar to mine, so she found this overly cognitive approach very difficult for her, too.

We tried to talk to the group about our need for sharing personal experiences and opinions and feelings in addition to hearing experts. But the majority of the participants were German history teachers who seemed to be comfortable with the program. A couple of them told us directly that they were not interested in sharing personal information, at least not publicly in the group. We organized an informal meeting after dinner for anyone interested in sharing their thoughts and feelings about the trip. The only person who came was one of the leaders.

I began to think that something was wrong with me. I couldn't make sense of what was going on. No one was speaking with me in a way that I could understand. I was having a different emotional experience than the others, or at least it seemed that way, and they didn't seem interested, or able to understand, why I was feeling the way I was.

On the third day, we went to Auschwitz. Because there were so many other groups like ours touring the site, we each had a wireless headset so that we could listen to the guide assigned to our group. I turned off the sound and decided to experience the camp without the voice of our guide. Listening to him distracted me. I continued to wear the headphones, partly to hide the fact I wasn't listening to our guide, and partly to block the noise from other groups. Although it was painful to be at Auschwitz, it was also strangely peaceful, and I experienced Auschwitz at a visual and emotional level, without words.

The day after our visit to Auschwitz, we were scheduled to hear two lectures after breakfast: one by a member of our group, Johannes, who I had come to like and respect, and one by a Polish historian. I walked into our meeting room and I started to have a panic attack. My heart started pounding, and my breathing became shallow and fast. I chose a seat next to an open window, where I could get some fresh air. The feeling of panic subsided a little bit, but I could feel my stomach tightening. I sat quietly and tried to calm myself by focusing on my breathing.

Everyone found a seat, and we were ready to begin. Someone closed the door to the room, and a woman sitting behind me promptly stood up and closed the window next to me. I felt a weight on my eyes and a lethargic feeling in my body. I turned around and tried to tell her that the room was warm and I would like some fresh air—but she interrupted me and firmly said that she wanted the window shut. "Do you want me to freeze?"

I didn't respond.

My wife was sitting next to me and sensed what was going on. She quietly told me to ignore the woman behind me. My wife knows that I overreact sometimes. I leaned over and quietly told her, "I may have to leave the room. Don't worry." I focused again on my breathing.

One of the leaders of our group introduced the morning program. I asked her if there would be a break between the two lectures. I needed to know when I would be able to leave the room. She said that they could take a break between the two talks, and I said, "Yes, please." When I found out that I would only have to sit for an hour and a half, I relaxed a little.

Johannes gave his lecture first. Although he was planning on reading from a prepared text, he began by describing his personal experience with Auschwitz. I perked up and thought that maybe there was a place here for my experience and perspective. His talk was short and interesting to me—the theme was the different perspectives people have about Auschwitz.

When the question and answer period came, I was the first to raise my hand. I decided to use English, and I began my question by accounting for the fact that I may have not understood what he was saying, and that my question might sound stupid. Johannes first reassured me that my question was a good question, and then answered me. While I have no memory of the question I asked, or his response, what I clearly remember is how respectful he was in his response to me.

We took a break, and I walked outside. I was feeling more at ease, and ready for the next lecture. I went back into the room. The room felt more open, and safe.

When the Polish historian gave his lecture, he talked to us without using a prepared text. I had a sense that he was in contact with us, and this, along with the fact that he was using a second language, made all the difference to me. I got excited and was fully engaged in what he was saying.

As he talked about the experiences that Polish people have had with Germans, he shared personal stories, his own and those that he has heard from family, friends, and colleagues. He presented Polish history as a composite of national, community, and family histories, whereas some of the German history teachers in our group talked as if history is only about facts, and purely objective. At one point he laughed at himself. I didn't see any of the history teachers in our group doing that.

Instead of feeling inferior to most of the members of our group, I felt equal to him. We were both outsiders here. We were both using a second language. We shared a similar style of teaching and learning.

I felt something similar when a German priest living in Auschwitz met with us and simply shared his thoughts, in a very slow and nonlinear way. Some of the members of our group didn't like his presentation because it was not linear and he didn't directly answer their questions. But that was what I liked about him: he simply told us what he was thinking as it occurred to him.

There were still two days left in the program and more lectures although we had left Auschwitz and were now in Krakow. I skipped some of the lectures, walked around the city by myself, and tried to spend less time with the group. When I was apart from the group, I was able to make sense of my experience.

I remembered something that I had often heard from people in marginalized groups in the U.S.: that self-blaming, being on guard for the danger that a group represents, being hyperaware of my surroundings—all of that can be a reaction to the experience of being an outsider and not fitting into the majority culture. It is a normal reaction. I was not crazy.

Later, in a conversation with my wife, I wondered: how much of my sense of panic, when I felt trapped in the room before Johannes's lecture, was due to the fact that we had just visited Auschwitz? And if I was having this emotional experience, then I wonder what it is like for Germans who have to live with the legacy of the Holocaust. My wife suggested that objectivity might be a protection against this pain, and yet, unfortunately, might also have led to the Holocaust in the first place. How else to explain a highly technical solution to killing millions of people? She believes that German history teachers need to have the skill to talk about feelings, and be able to examine their own emotional reactions to the past, when they are teaching about the Holocaust.

Two months after we returned from Poland, my wife and I invited two of the organizers of the trip to dinner at our apartment. We wanted to tell them how we experienced the trip. As usual, I cooked, and they complimented me on the food. They listened and asked questions and appreciated us taking the time to share what was emotionally difficult for us. They wanted to understand.

I decided on this evening to use both English and German. In planning for this conversation, my wife encouraged me to use both languages, to focus more on saying what I needed to say, rather than being understood. I wanted to let go of the unpleasant feelings I still had about the trip. I know from experience that these kinds of feelings will dissipate if I can fully express what I am feeling, and if I believe that I have been heard.

It worked. I felt relief by the end of the evening. They had heard me.

One of the things I told them is how overwhelmed I felt by the academic tone and the intellectual conversations between participants. The Akademikerdeutsch was simply too high for my ability, and there was too much of it for me to process. This surprised them. They forgot that I was using a second language because they experienced me as having a very high level of German fluency.

I heard the compliment and I wondered: was I regressing to my old behavior of acting like I understand when I don't? Or are they so used to being with other academics and intellectuals that they didn't recognize my differences and "see" me for who I am? Both of those things could be true, and it could be something else, too.

I have spent years listening to people and trying to understand them. I first learned to do that in English, and I have used this skill again and again in German even when I haven't understood the words being spoken. I focus all of my attention on the person who is speaking, and I pick up information from many sources: the tone of their voice, the expression on their face, the energy in their body, and my own feelings as I am with them. Even though they may not be aware of all the ways I am listening, I suspect that people notice that I am listening to them carefully and then assume that I understand.

Even though this trip was not pleasant, I am glad I went. I felt very close to my wife—we really supported each other during the trip. I learned some things about German and Polish history. I had the opportunity to visit Auschwitz.

I experienced how cognitive the German educational system is, and the impact of that on the expression of feelings and personal experiences in German culture, especially in academic settings. It helps me understand and put into context why I sometimes feel so out of place here, when I try to share my feelings and personal experiences.

As long as I live here and participate in educational programs, I will have to listen to lectures. It seems to be one of the primary ways that Germans share information in formal situations. I see this again and again as I attend forums and seminars in Nürnberg—lectures given by so-called experts followed by a question and answer period. I don't like this method, and I certainly don't ever want to subject myself again to sitting day after day in lectures.

But because of this trip to Poland, I learned that I could tolerate situations like these. I could get through them and arrive safely back home.

Cooper Thompson

Intimacy

I'm ambivalent about the title of this chapter. But I can't find a better word to describe an experience that is becoming more frequent the longer I am here: I'm in a conversation with someone, we're using German, and I feel a sense of intimacy. For many people intimate means sexual, but for me, intimate means being honest, sharing feelings, being present, listening, being truly interested in what we each have to say.

I had a conversation like this one day at the former site of the Nazi Party rallies in Nürnberg. By my standards, it was intimate. The really strange thing was, the young man I was talking with appeared to be a neo-Nazi.

My wife had helped organize a Peace Run for about 2,000 young people, and I was a volunteer. Girls and boys between the ages of 7 and 17 were running to raise money for global peace projects. They were doing laps in front of the massive granite podium on which Hitler had spoken at the annual rallies, an event documented in the film *Triumph of the Will*. My wife and her co-organizers had selected this site with the intent to symbolically transform the space.

My task was much more mundane: filling cups with water for the thirsty runners. Suddenly, Martina, another volunteer, came running up to me.

"Cooper, you have to come over here right away. There's a very strange guy, and we have to watch him carefully." I could hear the panic in her voice. This sounded serious, so I left my station and followed her.

About 20 meters away, in the middle of a small crowd of spectators, was a young man dressed in military style clothes. He was 16 or 17 years old. It looked to me like he was simply watching the runners.

But Martina whispered in my ear, "He's a neo-Nazi. Stand close to him and don't let him out of your sight." She had already recruited another volunteer, so now it made three of us who were standing within a couple of meters of him and watching his every move.

I didn't know the protocol in a situation like this, so I simply did what Martina and the other volunteer were doing. I assumed that they knew best, even though what we were doing felt a little odd to me.

I hadn't met any neo-Nazis although I had seen some in Nürnberg. I am sure that some are dangerous, but this guy didn't look very threatening to me. I was frankly curious about why he was here. I wanted to know his story.

So, after five minutes of surveillance, I decided on a different tactic. I was going to talk with him.

I walked closer to him. "Hi. I'm curious: why are you here?" I decided to be friendly and direct.

"A girl I know is running today, and I came to watch her." It didn't sound very suspicious to me.

I was even more surprised at what he said next. "I wish I could run with her, but I'm not registered."

"That's not a problem," I said. "You and I can run together. You want to?"

"But I'm wearing boots."

"I'm wearing sandals. That makes us kind of equal. We're not dressed the right way, but who cares?"

"Okay, let's run."

We joined the other runners.

"By the way, what's your name?"

"Max. What's yours?"

"Cooper."

"Where do you come from? You're not German."

I told Max why I was living in Germany, and then asked him what he was doing.

"I'm done with school, and I'm looking for a job. But it's hard to find one. I wasn't smart enough to go to a university or college, and I haven't done an internship, so I am not qualified to get a good job."

I knew a little bit about the school system, and what he said was exactly what I had heard: if someone only has a high school degree, and hasn't gotten a decent internship, then their chances in the job market are slim. I felt sad that he had come to the conclusion that he wasn't smart, so I empathized with him.

"I don't think the school system here is fair. There should be opportunities for everyone. I wish that you had an opportunity to get a good job."

"What's it like in the U.S.?" Max asked me, and I tried to explain some of the myths about equality in the U.S. and how social class determines educational and career opportunities. Max listened carefully and began to tell me what he knew about the history of the U.S. He knew a lot. I listened to him and told him that how impressed I was with what he knew.

We continued to run laps. There was a question I had, and when there was a pause in our conversation, I asked it.

"Are you a neo-Nazi?"

"I've gone to their meetings. They give me beers, and we talk about stuff. It's interesting."

"But are you actually a member? And aren't you dressed like you're a neo-Nazi?"

"No, I'm not really a member. I dress this way to provoke people. I know that it makes some people uncomfortable."

"Like the other volunteers, before we starting talking?"

"Yeah, that was funny. I moved a couple meters, and they followed me."

"You knew what was going on?"

"Of course. I wanted to see what would happen."

"But then I screwed it up and started to talking with you."

We both started laughing together.

"You know," I told him, "in some ways, we're similar. We're both outsiders here."

He agreed, and we talked for a few minutes about the similarities between being working class and being an immigrant.

Max's friend was finished running, and he went over to see her. He introduced us, and because they seemed like they wanted to talk, I decided it was time for me to go back to serving water. I told Max that I had enjoyed talking with him. He said that he had, too. We shook hands, and I turned and walked away.

I found my wife and told her what I had been doing for the past half hour. I was surprised to hear that she knew Max. He sometimes attended programs that she organized. She confirmed that he has gone to neo-Nazi meetings and likes to be provocative in his dress. Like me, she didn't experience him as threatening but, instead, someone who was labeled a failure in the school system and is now a lost soul trying to find a place where he belongs. That had been my assumption about some neo-Nazis, maybe not the leaders, but certainly some of the followers.

A year later, at the next year's Peace Run, I reminisced with one of the volunteers about my conversation with Max. She also knew him, and had the same perspective as my wife and I. In fact, Max was a volunteer for a project she organized.

"What is he doing now? I asked.

"He joined the Army. He couldn't get a job. He didn't have any other options."

"I think it's the wrong place for him. He won't get the job skills he needs."

"I agree. The problem is that there are neo-Nazis in the Army. I'm afraid that he will get involved with them again and this time more seriously."

I felt sad. I had only spent a half hour with Max, but I felt like we had both tried to learn a little about each other. I worry about him, and I hope that he's okay.

* * * * *

Right before I moved to Germany, an old friend said to me, "In six months you'll be sitting in a café somewhere, talking to someone in German, and feeling at home." He was being very optimistic.

Instead of the six months that he had predicted, it was a few years after I moved here when I was sitting in a café and having a conversation that, by my standards, felt like I was "at home." It was again at Café Fatal, and I was with Berndt.

The first few times he and I met, I was nervous and shy, not trusting my ability to communicate, asking lots of questions and listening rather than talking. But over time I felt more comfortable and talked more. This time, we talked about the meaning of home, how to keep excitement in a long term romantic relationship, what we had learned from our partners.

After a couple of hours, I got up the courage to ask him: "Is it boring to talk with me? I need to know that, because I'm afraid it is, since I use simple vocabulary, and I speak slowly. I'm sure it's sometimes hard to listen to me and understand me."

He reassured me: "No, I enjoy our conversations. It's easy to listen to you, and I can understand you." Then I suddenly remembered my friend's prediction and smiled to myself.

A few weeks later, I went to Berndt's house to have dinner with him and his friend Karl Heinz. We spent four hours together talking about our relationships with men and our observations about how men are socialized in the U.S. and in Germany. As I left at 11:15 p.m. and walked to the train station, I thought, *This is amazing. I just spent four hours with them, and I really enjoyed it.*

Germans have told me that it takes a long time to get to this level in a friendship. I've felt impatient at times about that, in comparison with how quickly a relationship can be established in the U.S. We might be more superficial in the U.S., but at least when I lived there, I had people to talk with.

In comparison to my attempts with Germans, I found it easier, in general, to develop friendships with other immigrants. Speaking German with them had a different quality than speaking German to native speakers. I felt like we were on the same level in our language ability, and we shared some similarities as outsiders. Although I know it's a generalization, I found other immigrants to be warmer and more outgoing than Germans, at least some of the time.

At the wedding of one of my wife's friends, one-third of the guests were immigrants. When I walked in and saw the diversity of the group, I felt both relaxed and excited. It was one of the first times I had been to a party where I wasn't alone as the only immigrant. A man from Egypt and I started talking in German, and right away I felt a connection with him. Even though we were strangers, I felt close to him. Then I talked with a man from India, again in German. Again, I felt close. Same thing with a woman from Turkey.

I can imagine for many people, the feeling of closeness that I am describing would make them feel uncomfortable. With me, it's the opposite. The more intimate the conversation, the more comfortable I feel. If I believe that we are actually meeting each other as human beings and that my conversation partners are really listening to me and interested in what I have to say, then I trust that they will be patient with me when I can't find the right words to express my thoughts and feelings.

If I trust them, then I have energy to think about how to say what I want to say instead of worrying about what they think of me and my German. So, it increases my self confidence in speaking German.

Regardless of how intimate our conversations are, if we are speaking German, I try to give my full attention to the people I am talking with. I try to understand them as best as I can. I want them to reciprocate. I want their full attention, and I want them to try to understand me.

* * * * *

I continued to go sporadically to the men's discussion group. One evening, there were 12 middle aged white German men there. I knew some of them from previous meetings, others were strangers. We had a lively and deep conversation about our experiences with relationships, addiction, and spirituality. I think I understood about 90% of what they said. I participated in the conversation, and shared my experiences, feelings, and thoughts. The other men listened to me, sometimes nodded in agreement, and later referenced something I had said. When I couldn't find the words for something, I felt comfortable enough to ask the group, and someone helped me.

I didn't have the experience on this night of comparing myself as "less than" to the other men, as I had done before. I knew that I was different from them, but that's all it was. There was no judgment attached.

After the meeting, Wolfgang asked me if we could meet sometime. I had noticed that he had been listening carefully as I talked about my experience with addiction, and so I was not surprised when he told me that he suspected that he might have a similar addiction and wanted to tell me about his experience. I said, "Sure, let's meet," and waited for him to get back to me.

A month later, he called me, and we met at Café Fatal. His first question was, "How much do you understand German."

I was glad he had asked, and I used his question to do something that I had rarely done so directly: I told tell him what would be helpful and not helpful as he talked to me. "Please don't use dialect, use standard German, and speak clearly and slowly."

He understood completely, having spent some time traveling in the U.S. and trying to use English. He had felt irritated when people talked too fast and used slang.

The time went by quickly. I was surprised when I looked up at the clock and saw that we had been talking for two hours.

As we were wrapping up our conversation, he complimented me on my ability to pay attention. Later, I realized that I was more or less counseling him, in German. It was another moment when I was amazed at what I could do in this language.

About a month after I met with Wolfgang, I had my regular meeting with a group of German psychotherapists. I had started a counseling practice for native English speakers living in Nürnbeg, and I used this group for supervision. We had been getting together for a couple of years to share our experiences working with clients.

On this evening, Nina asked me if she could refer a client to me. "Cooper, I think you could help him."

"But he's German, yes? I'd have to speak German with him."

"Yeah," she said casually.

"But my German is not good enough."

"Your German is good enough."

"Really?"

"Yes, really. You can work in German with clients."

"But I can't express subtle things, and I speak so slowly."

"Simple is good, and speaking slowly is good. Speaking slowly gives more space for thoughts and feelings. If clients need to speak slower with you, then they will be able to hear their thoughts and notice their feelings. When we speak quickly, we don't give thoughts and feelings a chance to be expressed."

"I'll think about it."

I decided not to work with him, but within a few months, a German couple asked me to help them with some difficulties they were having in their relationship. This time, I said "Yes." After several sessions, in which they spoke German and I spoke a mix of German and English, they told me how helpful our sessions were. We continued to meet, and on more than one occasion, they told me, "You're good."

* * * * *

After several years of occasional worrying if my wife might get pregnant and repeated conversations in which we agreed that we definitely didn't want children, we decided that I would get a vasectomy. Actually, I had thought about this for at least 20 years. A part of me wanted a vasectomy long before I met my wife, but I never got around to it. Or maybe I really didn't want a vasectomy. Maybe I was scared or held on to the idea of having kids.

I had already met with a urologist for a routine prostate screening and felt comfortable with him, so I asked him to go ahead and cut my *vas deferens*. We scheduled a date.

I also asked him if I could use his first name and if I could use *du* with him, and he said, "Of course."

For a week prior to the operation, at least once a day, my wife asked me if I was feeling nervous about it. I wasn't. I hadn't really thought about it much, but clearly she was nervous.

On the day of the appointment, she wanted to come with me. I didn't really think she needed to be there because it would be a routine 20-minute procedure, but she wanted to. We sat together in the waiting room for a few minutes, and then Monica, Michael's assistant, came in to get me. She was friendly, and I liked her immediately. She asked my wife if she wanted to watch the procedure. "No, no," she said emphatically. "I want to be nearby, but not that close." Monica acted like she was disappointed, but she was being playful with us. So, my wife sat in the waiting room while I followed Monica down the hallway.

Michael told me to undress and put on a gown, and he chatted with Monica while I was changing. It sounded like they are old friends; they were talking about a movie they had seen. I felt relaxed about getting sterilized. But as I lay on the table with my legs spread, Michael shaving my scrotum, Monica getting the scalpel and bandages ready, I began to feel a little nervous. My solution was to start a conversation.

I asked questions that most people would have asked before the operation, when they were discussing the possibility of getting sterilized.

"So, what you are actually going to do?"

Michael described the procedure as he injected me with a local anesthetic.

"And how long will it take?"

"Oh, 15 to 20 minutes, and then you need to lie here for another ten minutes or so before you can leave."

"Could you tell my wife that? She's sitting in the waiting room. I think she might want to know. She's a little nervous."

"I'll go out and tell her." Monica left and came back a couple of minutes later. "I told her. She said she wasn't leaving."

While we were waiting for the anesthetic to work, I asked them if they ever had other clients from the U.S.

"Yeah, sometimes," said Michael. He turned to Monica. "Remember those three soldiers who walked in the office one day without an appointment? And they all wanted to get vasectomies?"

"And do you remember," added Monica, "the guy from the U.S. who had been on a beach in Greece, got bitten in his scrotum by a bee, and his testicles swelled up?"

"No, you're kidding," I said. "What, he was on a nude beach?"

"Yeah, and when the poor guy came to us a week later, he was still swollen and mad at the Greek doctor who had treated him."

By this point we were all laughing. This was more like being at a party than lying in a doctor's office.

The anesthetic had done its job, and it was time to get down to business. Monica handed the scalpel to Michael. He made a small incision to get access to one of my *vas deferens*.

"What are you doing now?" I asked. I could feel something, like a little tug, but since I was lying down, I couldn't see what they were doing, and I was curious. Monica held a mirror for me to watch as Michael poked around and located the tube he wanted to cut.

"How many times have you done this operation?"

They looked at each other for the answer.

"Well, we've been working together for about 10 years, right?" said Monica.

"Yeah, that sounds about right," Michael answered.

"Maybe we've done a couple a hundred" Monica said to me.

I have no idea where my next question came from. It suddenly came out of my mouth, as if the devil had taken possession of me.

"So," I asked Monica, "You've seen a lot of balls in your life."

She grinned and said, "I dream of balls."

I cracked up laughing, which was a good thing, because in the next instant Michael pulled on my second *vas* in such a way that I felt pain in my abdomen.

"Ouch," I said. "What are you doing?"

He apologized and told me that this *vas* was a little difficult to get to. But he finally cut and tied it, then stitched me up. They cleaned up—there was a little bit of blood. I lay in peace for ten minutes, after which Michael checked on me, and told me I could go.

My wife was relieved to see me. We laughed on the way home about the conversation I had. She thought I was crazy. She would never have had that conversation. "But what was I going to do? I was lying there with my legs spread. I needed to talk with them."

My wife just shook her head. I told others about my adventure. They listened and also shook their heads.

Trusting Myself

January 15, 2009

It was a typical German winter day. It had been continuously below freezing for two weeks. The snow left on the roads had turned black. The air was damp, and the sky was grey. I don't like the cold, and the colors of the snow and sky made me wish that winter would pass quickly.

But I felt energized. I was on my way to a Yoga class.

For years, I had thought about doing Yoga again. When I was 23 and living in Good Thunder, Minnesota, I took a Yoga class with an older, white-haired woman.

The next year, in 1974, when I was teaching at an experimental school, I taught Yoga twice a week. A dozen or so children from 7 to 17 came voluntarily during their lunch break. I led them through a relaxation process and then some poses. Most of the students came regularly and were really interested in learning Yoga, even the little ones. A few students came simply because it was a quiet space, and if they wanted to sit quietly, or lie down, even sleep, that was fine with me.

As I walked to the community center where the class would be held, I checked in with my feelings, as I often did when I was getting ready to be in an unfamiliar setting and with people I didn't know. In the past, I sometimes had second thoughts just before I was leaving the house and on my way to a new group, or workshop, or talk. I worried if I would be able to understand and express myself, and if people would listen to me and accept me for who I am. Today, though, I was feeling confident.

I walked into the room—I was the first person there—and Gisela, the teacher, greeted me. She was maybe 75 years old, barely five foot tall, white hair like mine, full of energy. She hugged me as if I were an old friend and immediately told me how excited she was that I would be taking this course. In her 20 years of teaching Yoga, a man was a rare sight in her classes. She was quick to tell me that, amazingly, another man had registered for this course.

I think she wanted to reassure me that I wouldn't be the only man in a group of women. Although I didn't need reassurance about that—it was not uncommon for me—I probably did need a little reassurance that I would be welcome in her group. Her enthusiasm and affection put me at ease. Perhaps the sense of *déjà vu* was reassuring to me. Not only did she look a little like my first Yoga teacher, but also the weather reminded me of Minnesota in the winter.

Four women soon showed up for the class. They seemed to know each other. Gisela introduced me to them; one of them referred to me as Herr Cooper, using the formal *you*. I gently corrected her and told her that Cooper is my first name. This happened frequently: Cooper is an unusual first name so Germans often assumed that it's my last name.

The women looked to be middle class and about my age, and it was unusual in my experience that women of this age and class felt comfortable from the start using *du* with a male stranger. So, although I had suggested we use *du*, no one, except for Gisela, was calling me Cooper or using *du*. We would be meeting every week for two months, and it might take that long to become informal. Or maybe it would remain formal.

Gisela had arranged the mats in a circle. We each chose a place, and she began with some relaxation exercises. We sat and focused on our breathing. This was familiar to me. Although I didn't understand every word Gisela was saying, I didn't think I needed to. I used a strategy that I often used: filling in what I didn't know based on my previous experience. I knew what she was asking us to do, or at least I was pretty sure that I knew.

The fact that we were doing relaxation techniques made it easier for me to listen and understand. When I didn't understand a word or phrase or sentence, instead of tensing up, and trying to figure out what Gisela was saying, I simply relaxed and trusted that it would all make sense in the end. Or it wouldn't, and it wouldn't matter to me. The important thing was that I was in this class, taking Yoga, doing something that I had wanted to do for a long time, and I was doing it in German.

Half an hour later, as we were doing some poses, I really didn't understand the instructions that Gisela was giving. So I simply stayed in the pose I had, rather than changing poses as the others seemed to be doing.

Gisela walked by me and again said something I didn't understand, and again I didn't change my pose. As a way to account for not understanding her, I used one of my survival phrases I had created for myself when I first began to learn German: "Gisela, you know, sometimes I'm a little slow in German. I need a bit more time to understand."

Gisela's response surprised me. She told the group, "Cooper is doing exactly what I want you to do: go at your own pace. Slow is good. We go too fast in this life."

A few minutes later, as she was giving us instructions for another pose, Gisela told us, "Don't compare yourself to others; do only what you feel is comfortable for you. Be gentle with your body." I suddenly remembered the Theatre Games workshop and how reassured I felt when Stefan told us that we had a right and a responsibility to do only what we wanted to do.

I thought to myself: why can't we do this with language learning? How liberating it would be if a teacher emphasized the uniqueness of each student's journey toward language acquisition. What if students were told, "Go at your own pace. Take your time speaking. There's no need to rush. Take breaks if you are feeling overwhelmed. Notice the process you're going through. Appreciate your own particular progress and your challenges. It doesn't matter what other students can do in the target language; what matters is where you are, where you want to go, and how you get there."

After class, as I was walking back home, I wondered if I could find a Yoga course in Spanish or Turkish. I had always wanted to be fluent in Spanish. I'd like to learn Turkish because there are so many Turkish immigrants here. Yoga would be a great way for me to learn another language.

Then my mind came back to earth, and I realized I probably wouldn't find a Yoga class in Spanish or Turkish, at least not in Nürnberg. I was simply feeling optimistic. Maybe it was the Yoga at work on my soul.

*****

Later that year, I attended a presentation of a new project in Nürnberg that was helping young immigrants deal with discrimination they face in the workplace. There were about 75 people at the event. Most of them had some professional connection with this kind of work or were representatives of corporations, foundations, and agencies who funded and supported this project.

The program was very formal and polite, filled with congratulatory statements by the project's sponsors. Some of the immigrant youth from the project were in the audience and briefly came on stage to introduce themselves, but it seemed to be a time for the adults to speak.

I wondered why immigrant youth were playing such a small role. Maybe this was a cultural difference, or maybe I was glorifying the U.S., but in my recollection, a presentation like this in the U.S. would have been dominated by young immigrants sharing their experiences with racism and xenophobia. There would have been comments about the history of immigration and systemic patterns of discrimination.

Then a very curious thing happened. The stage was cleared. A table and three chairs replaced the podium and microphone. Posters of Greece were put on the walls. The stage became a travel agency. Three German actors began performing.

One of them played the owner of the travel agency, a Greek immigrant, about 50 years old, who had been in Germany for decades. A second actor played an intern at the travel agency. She was about 20, also an immigrant, but from the former Soviet republic of Georgia. The third actor played a German client, white skinned, middle class, middle aged woman. She wanted to visit Greece and had asked the agency to put together an itinerary. The intern got the assignment and was presenting it to the client for her approval.

It seemed to be going well—the client was excited to see the sights, and the intern made adjustments based on the client's preferences—but then the owner started to interrupt and take over the presentation. He wanted the best for his client and was proud of what his country could offer and his local connections. He seemed unaware of the impact of his behavior on the intern, who was clearly uncomfortable with the way the owner was dominating the situation.

The play grabbed my attention and the attention of the audience. But I was vaguely uncomfortable as I watched the scene unfold on stage. Three German actors and two were "playing" immigrants. An older man dominating a younger woman. A largely white German audience watching a conflict between two immigrants. I was getting agitated. Something was missing here. The play was focusing on an interpersonal conflict between the owner and the intern that clearly involved sexism and adultism, but the play did not seem to be addressing systemic discrimination against immigrants in the workplace, which was the goal of the project being presented here.

When the play was finished, the actors asked the audience for their opinions. A white German woman said something about how typical the Greek immigrant was—"I know this type," she said, critically—and was asked to come on stage and play him as she would like him to be.

She at first resisted, then agreed, climbed onto the stage, and played a very collaborative supervisor. The intern and client were happy. The audience applauded.

The actors again turned to the audience. A white German man suggested negotiation between the owner and the intern. He climbed on stage and tried that and was not very successful. The frustration of the owner began to show, that his expertise and old fashioned values were not appreciated in 2009. He didn't want to negotiate with the intern. He wanted to teach her what he knew from experience.

Then I raised my hand to make a comment. I was nervous, afraid that I wouldn't be able to say in German what I was thinking. Strangely, it had not occurred to me that I might end up on stage as a consequence of making a comment. I was simply aware of needing to say something about how the actors and audience were focusing too much on the Greek man as the problem and not enough on the experience of immigration and the problem of German attitudes and policy toward immigrants.

One of the actors noticed me and approached me with the microphone.

"Would you like to say something?" she asked.

"Yes, but German is not my native language. I don't know if the audience here will understand me."

"That's not a problem. Please, go ahead."

"I am an immigrant, too. I see this situation differently. I don't think the Greek immigrant is the problem. I think the problem is how Germany deals with immigrants. I've heard many immigrants talk about how difficult it is for them to live here. I think you need to tell the story about his experience as an immigrant instead of the problems between him and his intern."

Of course, I was invited on stage.

"But my German is not good enough," I said to the actor.

"Your German is good enough," she responded.

Without being fully aware of what I was doing, I made the decision to get on stage. As I stood up, I turned to the audience and said, "You have to watch out what you say around here." They laughed. I had quickly become an actor. This was not unfamiliar to me. I had spent many years in front of groups, but never had I acted in a play. Never had I spoken to an audience of strangers in German.

"Do you want to have a conversation with the intern or the client?" the actor asked me.

"No, I want to talk with someone who can understand my experience as an immigrant. Maybe a German, maybe another immigrant." I paused. "An immigrant. Yes, I want to talk with another immigrant."

She asked for a volunteer from the audience. A Russian woman offered to come on stage with me.

The actor asked me to set the scene. I arranged two chairs so that they were facing each other, turned to the audience, and said, "We're at my house, sitting in my living room. She is a friend." I turned to her. "Would you like a glass of water?"

"Yes, thank you."

I walked off stage to get her a glass of water. I was being a good host and a good actor. Again, the audience laughed.

I handed her the glass and took my seat. "Thanks for coming to my house," I told her. "You know, my experience here in Germany has been difficult. Perhaps you can understand. You are an immigrant like me."

I described some of the difficulties I had had with learning German, with the German bureaucracy, with the rigid German culture, and with German people. "I hear similar things from other immigrants. They have tried to learn German, but they are never good enough. They are frustrated. Their job skills and educational experience is not recognized here. And they say that the people in Nürnberg are unfriendly!" That comment stimulated a reaction from the audience: I heard some people laughing, but it sounded like nervous laughter. I also heard a few gasps, as if to say, "He didn't say that, did he?"

Then I turned to my friend on stage and asked her, "What is your experience as an immigrant?" She described experiences that were similar to mine and other immigrants. We continued talking for several more minutes.

At a pause in our conversation, the actor ended the scene, thanked us, and asked the audience to applaud. They did. I left the stage and took my seat. There was a short discussion that followed, but I didn't hear any of it. I was absorbed in my own thoughts and feelings. I was physically there, but my mind was somewhere else.

The actors announced a coffee break. There would be refreshments in the next room. As I stood up, I looked around for a familiar face, for someone to talk to. I was suddenly feeling very isolated and needed some support. I wanted to talk about what had just happened.

I tried a Turkish man sitting near me—we had met previously—but he needed to go talk to someone else. I tried a white German woman who worked with young immigrants—she had invited me to this presentation after we had met at another event—but she needed to prepare for what would come after the break. Both of them told me, briefly, that what I had said was good. But I needed something more, and I didn't know what it was. My intuition told me that they didn't want to talk with me. I wondered if I had done something wrong, or worse, if there something wrong with me.

I went to the coffee break room, walked around, hoping to find someone to talk with. I made eye contact with people, waited for a response that said, "I would like to talk with you," but got nothing. I picked up a glass of water and stood by myself near the wall. I was feeling lonely, scared that no one wanted to talk with me or be seen with me. Again I wondered what was wrong, and this time answered myself: it must have something to do with being an immigrant and the fact that my German is so bad.

Eventually, someone approached me. His first comment to me was, "I was shocked to hear you say that the people in Nürnberg are unfriendly." I nodded my head, and then introduced myself and asked his name. I wanted to hear what he had to say, but I didn't want to have this conversation without at least greeting each other and sharing our names.

Then I told him, "What I said about the people here being unfriendly, I hear this from many immigrants You haven't heard this?"

"No. Never. And I don't think we're unfriendly."

I tried to explain to him that there is a difference between perception and truth, that my comment about people in Nürnberg being unfriendly is the perception of many immigrants and not necessarily the truth. But I'm not sure he understood this, or perhaps I didn't explain it very well. He only heard my comment as a criticism of him personally.

Nonetheless, we continued to talk about our different perceptions of German culture. It was not easy. He was quite defensive, and he told me how immigrants need to adjust to living here. I agreed with him but couldn't get him to agree with what I was saying.

Toward the end of our conversation, he said, "I hope that I have changed your impressions of our culture."

"No, actually you haven't." In this conversation, he had confirmed some of my impressions: he had approached me without introducing himself, he didn't know much about the experience of immigrants, and he was defensive when I tried to tell him about our experiences.

Then he said something that really surprised me. "But I want to make the world a better place for you."

I responded, "I don't think you should make the world a better place for me. That's my responsibility. I think you should do that for yourself."

He had a puzzled look on his face.

I asked him, "Are there things that you don't like about this culture? Do you sometimes find it unfriendly?"

"Yes. Sometimes I think the people in Nürnberg are closed and cold."

"Then we agree on something."

"Yes."

"I have an idea. The next time there's a program like this, you volunteer to go on stage and tell other Germans what you think about this culture and what you would like to change. Then I would feel your support."

"I don't know if I could do that. That's hard."

"I know. I was just on stage. It was hard. But if I can do it in my second language, then I'm sure you can do it in your native language."

The coffee pause was over, and we were being called back to the conference room. I thanked him for our conversation. He looked puzzled that I would thank him. I knew it was a cultural difference or maybe just my habit to thank people, but I kept that to myself. We said goodbye.

Although the event was continuing, I left. I was emotionally drained. I had been performing the role of the Greek immigrant, when actually, it was my own story I was telling. I had told an audience of Germans, in German, about the pain of being an immigrant here. I was still feeling that pain. I needed some time away from this group of people and some time to think about what had happened.

As I rode my bike home, I realized that I probably offended some people with my comment about the unfriendliness of Germans. I could have said it more diplomatically. Maybe I was not polite and superficial like I was supposed to be at an event like this. Instead I had said some things that people might not want to hear. Some people might say I was being provocative. I think I was being outspoken. That didn't surprise me; it's not the first time I have spoken out when I was expected to stay quiet.

What did surprise me was the momentary shame I felt about being an immigrant and that I had told myself that my German was bad. I was forgetting that what I had just done required a pretty good grasp of German and that it required courage.

Within a few hours, the feeling of shame passed, and I was able to let go of the thought that my German was bad. When I told Karuna, my first German teacher and now a friend, about this experience, she said to me, "If you can describe your experience as an immigrant in this setting, then you are definitely fluent. Your German is good. There is nothing wrong with you. Germans' ability to understand you and their attitude toward immigrants are different issues."

I need to remember this when I start to distrust my ability to communicate in German.

* * * * *

A year prior to my acting debut as a Greek travel agent, I had traveled to the U.S. It was during this trip that I meet Dr. Rebecca Oxford, talked to her second language learning class, and learned that I was bilingual. It was also during this trip that I had opportunities to speak a little Spanish and learn some sign language in Italian.

At the University of Maryland, I ate lunch at a dining hall where there was a buffet. I approached the woman carving meat and asked her what kind of meat she was serving. She tried to tell me, in English, but her voice was hesitant, and she really wasn't able to describe how the meat had been prepared. She paused, took a deep breath, and said, with a touch of resignation in her voice, "It's meat. Just meat."

Because I heard what sounded like a Spanish accent, I asked her, in Spanish, if she spoke Spanish. She said, "Yes," and then I asked her in Spanish what the meat was. This time she gave me a detailed answer to my question, in a strong voice, and with obvious self-confidence.

I didn't understand completely what she told me, but I caught enough, and I certainly knew more about the meat I would be eating than I did when I asked her in English. More important, at least for me, I felt like I had made a little contact with her, and that felt better to me than a conversation in which she was at a loss for words. She gave me a portion of meat, and I enjoyed my meal even more because of our interaction.

If I think that I've lost a lot of French ability, I've lost even more Spanish. I took some Spanish courses at a community school in my 30's and never really used it in a Spanish-speaking country like I did with French. So, asking her if she spoke Spanish and what kind of meat was about my limit. Yet, I had switched to Spanish pretty spontaneously, without first thinking whether I could communicate with her in her language.

The next day, while staying a friend's house in Washington, DC, I met Alberto, a deaf Italian man. As soon as we were introduced, he wanted to talk with me. He could speak a little English, but it was not easy for me to understand his words. He wasn't inhibited about talking, so I felt inspired to try to talk with him.

Alberto signed and talked in a mix of Italian and English. I had always wanted to learn Italian, so maybe this was my opportunity. I used the only words I knew in Italian—*buon giorno* and *grazie* and Alberto took that as his cue to teach me some basic Italian and sign language. I learned—and subsequently forget—how to say and sign, "My name is Cooper, it's good to meet you, but sorry, I don't speak Italian." It wouldn't be my last opportunity to learn Italian.

The next summer, my wife and I were on our way to Corsica for a two week vacation. It was the fourth time we had gone there. As we drove through Italy, and stopped for the night in a village, I surprised myself, my wife, and the couple we were traveling with when I approached Italians on the street and asked for directions. Of course, I had forgotten what Alberto had taught me. But here I was, trying to talk with people who spoke a language that I didn't know. Miraculously, it worked. We were able to communicate. They used Italian, I used German, French, and English.

In Corsica, we stayed at a campsite where the staff were mostly French, the campers German, Italian, French, Dutch, and Swiss. The working languages were French, German, and English. I tried to use a mix of German and French and sometimes got confused, but we communicated.

At the campsite, I took a yoga course in French and understood, more or less, the teacher's instructions. I confronted two different men, in French, about the loud, late night music at their restaurants adjacent to the campsite. I made reservations on the phone when we decided to go to a different campsite. My French was not that good. I just felt confident using a second language.

Back in Nürnberg, I unexpectedly had an opportunity to put all of my languages to use. I was asked to lead a three day workshop for young people from eight countries: Germany, Austria, Luxembourg, Poland, Spain, France, Serbia, and Hungary. The topic would be racism, and the working language would be English.

The 15 participants had widely different levels of English fluency: a young Serbian man used slang that I would hear only from young people in the U.S. Two young German women spoke a pretty formal style of school English with a British accent. A young Polish woman spoke a little English but hesitantly. A young Hungarian man could understand but not speak English—he felt more comfortable using German—and similarly, a young French woman could understand English but preferred to speak French. A young man from Spanish spoke perfect English but not a word of German. Two young women from Luxembourg had it relatively easy: they could get by in French, German, or English.

I encouraged each participant to use the language that felt most comfortable to them, given the conversation and context. It was more important, I told them, to find their own voice, to say what they wanted to say, than to be understood. I trusted that we would find a way to understand each other. We did.

At one point, the Hungarian man was in a role play and had strong feelings about an issue. I encouraged him to speak Hungarian, and when he did, we heard his feelings clearly, even though we didn't understand the content of what he was saying. When he had been speaking German, we could hear the content but not the feelings.

Although I hadn't planned to do so, I became a translator at critical points. When the Austrians wanted to speak German, I translated into English. When the French woman wanted to speak French, I translate that also into English. A few times, I translated from English to French and German. It was a stretch for me, and other participants helped when I didn't know how to say something. Some of them were much more fluent than I was.

We did a feedback round. I encouraged each person to speak both in English and in their native language. It was wonderful to hear so many different languages in the room, and to hear how confident people felt using English, even those who had very limited ability. They were surprised at how well they had communicated with each other, and they expressed their gratitude for this opportunity to learn from each other. For three days, we had created a space where they were able to share their thoughts and feelings about racism, in whatever language they wanted to use, or could use.

* * * * *

The next month, I met a woman who had taught English and Norwegian for many years. I told her about my experience learning German, how difficult it had been for me, and she loaned me a book written in French about a unique method for learning a second language. The title was enough to hook me: *Psychodramaturgie Linguistique (PDL): Sur les Chemins d'une Pédagogie de l'Être*, by Bernard Dufeu.

This method uses psychodrama and is based on "who we are" (Être). This is exactly what I was missing in the German courses I took, where the material (grammar and vocabulary) was at the center of the process, and the learners (our feelings and identity) were ignored. Ironically, this method uses techniques that are similar to what I had experienced in my acting debut, techniques developed by Augusto Boal called *Theatre of the Oppressed*.

Online, I found an Italian course using the PDL method, offered in Köln, about a four hour train ride north of Nürnberg. I registered, and on a Friday afternoon in October, I walked into another world of language learning.

We were a group of five—four native German speakers from Köln, and me—lying on mats on the floor, listening to Nadja's soft voice, guiding us through a relaxation exercise. She told us, first in German and then Italian, to let the floor support each part of our bodies and allow the tension to dissolve. The instructions were repeated several times, with each part of our bodies. We did this at the beginning of each day that we met. We also did movement, rhythm games, and poetry. Nadja gave us instructions in both German and Italian. We spoke as much Italian as we could and used German when we needed to.

Then Nadja began working with each of us individually. I volunteered to be the first one. I was eager to see what would happen. I sat close to Nadja, wearing a mask so that I could concentrate and not get distracted by the other members of our group. They were sitting in a semicircle a meter or two away from us, listening carefully.

Nadja told me to focus on my breathing. Then she asked me to say a word that I had heard in Italian, a word that I liked or interested me. I had heard her use the word *libertà*, and I had understood from the context that it meant *freedom*.

So, I picked *libertà*, and Nadja told me to say it three times, with a different gesture and intonation each time I said it.

Then she improvised a short story in Italian with the theme *libertà*. I listened to it once. She told me the story a second time, pausing after each phrase while I tried to repeat exactly what she had said. We did the same thing one more time. Then we tried to have a brief conversation about *libertà*, using what I had heard in the story.

Each of us did this same process several times during the weekend, always with a different word and different story. I went from *libertà* to *bicicletta* (bicycle), where we took a ride together in the country, and eventually to *la cucina* (cooking and food), where we planned a meal together. Nadja gave me some dialogue to work with. I listened to her and tried to repeat exactly what she had said, and then we started to have a conversation.

Nadja began. "Let's cook together and invite some friends."

"Yes, yes. Let's cook together and invite some friends."

"What do you want to cook?"

"I want to cook pasta and fish."

Then Nadja said that she would bring ice cream for dessert.

"No, no." I cried out. "No ice cream."

She repeated, "No, no, I won't bring ice cream."

"I want you to bring ... " And I stopped, because I couldn't remember the word I had learned a couple of hours earlier: fig. So I made a little ball with fingers, put an imaginary fig in my mouth, made smacking, sensuous sounds with my lips, and said, "Delicious."

She looked puzzled. "I don't understand."

"Fruit. Red."

"Ah, figs! You want me to bring figs!"

"Yes, yes, I want you to bring figs!"

I loved it. I could be passionate and loud, and I got to decide what we talked about. Nadja's job as the teacher was to listen to me, teach me the words I wanted, and then support me as I tried to find my voice in Italian.

Of course, I made many mistakes, and it was hard work. I couldn't do this without her. At one point, Nadja told me, "Watching you was like watching someone have a baby." I was sweating and pushing to get Italian words out of my mouth. Still, the words did come out. I was able to have short conversations with Nadja, in Italian, a language that I had never spoken before the weekend.

I totally enjoyed it. I didn't want to stop on Sunday afternoon, even though I was exhausted from using both German and Italian.

Riding back on the train, I thought about what made this weekend so successful for me. I was relaxed instead of tense. We were a small supportive group. I trusted Nadja as a teacher. She seemed to want to understand me and cared about how I was feeling. I never felt criticized for not remembering or making mistakes. I, the learner, was the center of attention, instead of the teacher or the curriculum being the center of attention. I got individualized "lessons" based on storytelling and based on what I wanted to say. I had the chance to express my feelings in a new language. I played with words, as if I were a child learning my first language, and yet I was treated as an adult.

This was the approach to language learning that I had been searching for. The goal was communication, and we communicated in this method through contact with each other. It even felt intimate at moments.

A month later, Nadja called me on the phone to check on how I was doing. I told her that I wanted to learn more about PDL, and she told me about a 6-month training program to learn the techniques.

I registered. I wanted to learn how to teach English using PDL. I was eager to take more Italian lessons with Nadja. I haven't found anyone who can teach me Turkish or Spanish using PDL, but I'm looking.

* * * * *

As I was finishing this book, my wife told me that the name I had originally chosen as a pseudonym for my mother-in-law, Ilse, didn't really fit her. She wasn't an Ilse. I didn't understand my wife's reasons for this, but I believed her.

So I picked up the phone. It was often hard to reach Anna because she was in the barn, or the fields, or somewhere in the village. But it was a cold December evening, and I was pretty sure I would find her at home, most likely sitting by the wood stove in the kitchen.

"Hi, Anna, it's Cooper."

"Cooper! How are you?"

"I'm good, Anna. How are you?"

"Okay."

"Do you have much snow?" I asked. It had been snowing the last few days.

"Yeah, of course."

"How much?"

"About 20 centimeters. Is there snow in Nürnberg?"

"We have about 20 centimeters, too. And it's cold."

"Here, too."

"Anna, I have a question. You know I'm writing a book about my experience learning German."

"You are?"

"Yes. I didn't tell you that?"

"No."

"And you are in the book. I wrote some things about you."

"Really?"

"Yes, really. But I don't want to use your real name. I have been using Ilse, but your daughter says it's not the right name for you. So here's my question. What name would you like me to use?"

She paused. "I don't know." And then, "It doesn't matter."

"Are you sure?"

Another pause. "Anna. I want you to use Anna."

We talked for a few more minutes about our plans for the holidays. I asked her which day would be best for my wife and me to come to her house for a visit. I'm not sure if she understood what I was asking, or maybe I wasn't clear, or maybe I didn't understand her. By the end of the conversation, I didn't know what we had decided. But I didn't worry because I knew that my wife would be talking to her and figure it out.

When I got off the phone, I realized what I had just done. I had casually picked up the phone and called my mother-in-law. I hadn't hesitated. In fact, I had been excited to call her. I was curious to find out what name she would choose.

It was sweet to talk with her. On this night, I heard a softness and affection in her voice, something I hadn't really noticed before. I'm glad I called her.

REFERENCES

I read and re-read the following and found them very helpful in making sense of my experience using German and living in Germany:

Benson, Phil and Nunan, David (Eds.) (2004). *Learner's Stories: Difference and Diversity in Language Learning.* Cambridge: Cambridge University Press.

Ehrman, Madeline E. (1996). *Understanding Second Language Learning Difficulties.* Thousand Oaks, California: Sage Publications.

Norton, Bonny (2000). *Identity and Language Learning: Gender, Ethnicity, and Educational Change.* Harlow, England: , Pearson Education.

Pavlenko, Aneta et al. (2001). *Multilingualism, Second Language Learning, and Gender.* Berlin: Mouton de Gruyter.

Ross, Rupert (1996). *Returning to the Teachings: Exploring Aboriginal Justice.* Toronto: Penguin Books.

(Although at first glance this book has nothing to do with language, there is a chapter in the middle of the book, *Watch Your Language,* that introduced me to the idea that cultural values might be imbedded in language.)

Spohn, Cornelia (Ed.) (2006). *Zweiheimisch: Bikulturell Leben in Deutschland.* Hamburg: edition Körber-Stiftung.

I quoted from the following books:

Campbell, Don G. (1989). *The Roar of Silence.*, Wheaton, Illinois: Quest Books, the Theosophical Publishing House.

Ellis, Rob (1997). *Second Language Acquisition.* Oxford: Oxford University Press.

Farber, Barry (1991). *How to Learn Any Language: quickly, easily, and on your own!* New York: Barnes & Noble.

Hoffman, Eva (1989). *Lost in Translation*. New York: Penquin Books.

Mistry, Rohinton (1995). *A Fine Balance*. New York: Vintage International

Walker, Alice (1998). *By the Light of My Father's Smile*. New York: Random House.

Wolfe, Thomas (1947). *Look Homeward Angel*. New York: Charles Scribner's Sons.

About the Author

Cooper Thompson lives in Nürnberg, Germany. He is a counselor and coach (www.cooper-thompson.com), as well as being an elected representative on the Integration Council in Nürnberg and a member of Diversity Works, a German consulting group that helps individuals and organizations challenge discrimination (www.diversity-works.de). He is a co-author of *White Men Challenging Racism: 35 Personal Stories* (2003, Duke University Press) and the author of many essays and educational materials on oppression and privilege, the majority of which can be found on his website www.cooper-thompson.com/essays.

Other Books by MSI Press

Achieving Native-Like Second-Language Proficiency: Speaking

Achieving Native-Like Second-Language Proficiency: Writing

A Believer-in-Waiting's First Encounter with God

Blest Atheist

Communicate Focus: Teaching Foreign Language on the Basis of the Native Speaker's Communicative Focus

Diagnostic Assessment at the Distinguished-Superior Threshold

El Poder de lo Transpersonal

Forget the Goal: The Journey Counts...71 Jobs Later

How to Improve Your Foreign Language Proficiency Immediately

Individualized Study Plans for Very Advanced Students of Foreign Language

Losing My Voice and Finding Another

Mommy Poisoned Our House Guest

Puertas a la Eternidad

Road to Damascus

Syrian Folktales

Teaching and Learning to Near-Native Levels of Language Proficiency (Vol. 1-4)

Teaching the Whole Class

The Rise and Fall of Muslim Civil Society

Thoughts without a Title

Understanding the People Around You: An Introduction to Socionics

What Works: Helping Students Reach Native-like Second-Language Competence

When You're Shoved from the Right, Look to the Left: Metaphors of Islamic Humanism

Working with Advanced Foreign Language Students

Journal for Distinguished Language Studies (annual issue)

Losing My Voice and Finding Another